HOUSE

Upon The

SAND

HOUSE

Upon The

SAND

By Mark Clayton Peterson

HOUSE UPON THE SAND
Copyright 1999

First Publication 2000

To order single or multiple copies of this book call toll-free 1 (877) 882-6060. An operator will help you, or leave your name and phone number and we will call you back; OR you can send a check or money order for $14.00 U.S. per book ordered, made out to DawnStar Book Co. Send your order to DawnStar Book Co., P.O. Box 1800; Roosevelt, UTAH 84066. Please include your name, phone number and return mailing address with your check or money order. We will mail your book(s) to you. You can also contact us at our E-mail address (dawnstarbook@hotmail.com). Please leave your name and phone number and we will call you back to set up your order.

Published by: DawnStar Book Co.
Cover Design: Mark C. Peterson

ISBN: 1-890558-90-7

Printed in the United States of America

Acknowledgments

I wish to thank all my family for their continued support as I wrote this book. Especially, I wish to thank my wife, Vickie, for her great love and effort that made it possible for me to write this story as I did. I am also grateful to the many people who read the numerous rough drafts of this book and shared their ideas and encouragement.

My editor, Lauri Updike, helped a great deal as well, as she guided me to keep this book as fluid and grammatically correct as possible, in spite of myself. Last but not least, I need to thank the Lord and His prophets, who gave this information to us, so that we might know what is to come and how we can be prepared.

Dedication

I dedicate this book to my wife and children. May the blessings of the Lord rest upon them always.

Author's Note

This is a fictional work which presents prophecies which are not yet fulfilled. For that reason the people in the story (whether they be named individuals, political figures or public groups) are also fictional, and therefore cannot be construed to represent real people or groups, either private, public or political.

Contents

PREFACE

One of the most important events in the history of the world will be the second coming of Jesus Christ. Prophets since the time of Adam have looked with anticipation to His coming in glory. They have seen it in vision, and they have seen the events that lead up to it. They have written of these events as they yearned for a better day. Indeed, the prophetic writings about the second coming of Christ are numerous, so much so that they are often misunderstood due to the sheer volume of information available. It can be a daunting and confusing task to understand what each prophecy means, and to understand how all of these separate prophecies fit together appropriately in the time sequence of the events of the second coming.

There are hundreds of prophecies about the second coming of the Savior. The overwhelming majority of these prophetic utterances address only a small part of the vast array of events that must occur prior to our Lords coming. Like numerous pieces in a very large puzzle, each prophetic piece is generally clear, but is so small as to leave the person putting the puzzle together without a clear picture of what the final result will be. Only with meticulous study and work will the pieces begin to fit together, and then the finished picture finally appears. This book takes those prophetic puzzle pieces, puts them together, and paints a picture of what the completed puzzle might look like; i.e. what the events leading up to the second coming might look like, and how they might affect us. Notice, I said might look like. Many of the prophecies can fit together several different ways, and so I had to pick one of the potential combinations to write into this story. I picked those combinations and meanings that seemed the most reasonable to me at that time.

There are many current events that are happening that seem to fulfill prophecies on this topic, and probably will play a role in coming events. I have attempted to weave these current factual political, financial and spiritual realities into this fictional presentation in the way that they will probably fit. For example, Goals 2000 and School to Careers are laws that are already on the books, and in a small way are already starting to do what the book presents. These laws contain within them the actual powers mentioned by the book. These powers just have not yet been exercised to their full oppressive potential. Most people have never read these two laws and so do not realize what is in them. Perhaps unintentionally, some government representatives who are explaining these laws to the public are misrepresenting them. They are presenting these laws in ways that are not entirely true. This is occurring on many fronts at this time, not just with these two laws.

The same kind of potential for harm is found in financial events that are building now, such as the stock markets and hedge funds. The greatest tragedy of all is that people are ever more willing to compromise their standards in the name of expediency. More detailed and complete examples of these daily realities, and others, are mixed throughout the story. I have written the story in this manner to try and show how the fulfillment of these prophecies will have a very real day-to-day affect on our personal lives. We are personally going to be affected politically, financially and spiritually. These are not going to be events for some other generation. We are the ones who are going to feel this, and so we must prepare ourselves and our children. The prophets of the Lord have given us good counsel on how to do this, spiritually and physically.

This story covers those prophecies relating to the destruction of the wicked in North America. For that reason the picture painted here does not include all events leading to Christ's coming. The time frame chosen for the story was roughly two years. This was done for the convenience of the story, and was not derived from any prophetic source. The actual time that will elapse during this cleansing period could be longer or shorter than this. The general events in the story are derived from prophetic sources. This is also true of the general order of events.

Specifics in the story are not always prophetic in nature, since I did have to create characters and names and places to allow the story to flow. However, as much as I was humanly able to do, I have included every prophecy into this story that relates to this topic. I have drawn on volumes of information to do this. The main sources used were the scriptures; such as the *Bible,* and *The Book of Mormon-Another Testament of Jesus Christ,* and the *Doctrine and Covenants.* Secondarily, I also drew on the teachings of the modern prophets. I would strongly encourage all to go back and study these prophecies from their original sources. I have listed many of the places where these prophecies can be found in the appendix of this book. Please know that this list is not complete, but will be a good starting point. For those who do not have a *Book of Mormon-Another Testament of Jesus Christ,* or a *Doctrine and Covenants,* contact the missionaries of the Church of Jesus Christ of Latter-day Saints and they can get you copies of these two books and explain where they came from and what is generally in them. The real value of the Book of Mormon is its testimony of Jesus Christ. Secondarily, within its pages, it contains many prophecies of the future of America.

You will notice that no year was set for the beginning of this story. These events could start soon, or they could be years away. When they do begin, I expect them to unfold somewhat as they are portrayed in this fictional story.

This is a fictional work which presents prophecies which are not yet fulfilled. For that reason the people in the story (whether they be named individuals, political figures or public groups) are also fictional, and therefore cannot be construed to represent current real people or groups, either private, public or political.

Let me point out that this is not a book of scripture. It is not a complete catalog of all prophecies about the second coming of Jesus Christ. It is a fictional story about how the destruction of the wicked in America might unfold as it relates to prophecy and current political, financial and spiritual realities.

When people think of the prophecies about the second coming of Christ, they tend to fall into one of three groups.

First, there is the doomsday group, who focus in on all the trials and tribulations that are coming. Second, there is the "all is well in Zion" group, who have "buried their heads in the sand" as they claim that everything is okay, and think that things will just keep going as they are. Third, there is the group in the middle, who are aware that terrible trials are coming, but who are also aware that there is much good that is happening, and who also know that in the end even better things are coming. The key is to be righteous and endure to the end, and whatever you do, follow the prophet of the Lord Jesus Christ.

I hope this book will inspire those who read it to more diligently search the scriptures. I hope this book will motivate many people to get themselves ready for the time of trial ahead, as well as the marvelous blessings that will follow. Most important of all, I hope this book will open peoples' eyes to the need to repent of their sins and draw closer to their Heavenly Father and Jesus Christ.

CHAPTER 1

REMEMBRANCE

Nothing is so certain as change, or as unchanging as human nature. For good, or for ill, I have experienced the veracity of this truth over the last several years. As the tumultuous sands of time shifted beneath these United States, I saw all I knew, or thought I knew, crumble, as our lives were forced to settle on the bedrock of truth. So I write this remembrance of all that which happened. The cascade of those events poignantly reminds me of two ancient prophets, and their words.

Moroni 9:12-15 "(And only a few years have passed away, and they were a civil and a delightsome people) But O my son, how can a people like this, whose delight is in so much abomination-How can we expect that God will stay his hand in judgment against us? Behold, my heart cries: Wo unto this people. Come out in judgment, 0 God, and hide their sins, and wickedness, and abominations from before thy face!"

Mormon 6:16-20 "And my soul was rent with anguish, because of the slain of my people, and I cried: 0 ye fair ones, how could ye have departed from the ways of the Lord! 0 ye fair ones, how could ye have rejected that Jesus, who stood with open arms to receive you! Behold, if ye had not done this, ye would not have fallen. But behold, ye are fallen, and I mourn your loss. 0 ye fair sons and daughters, ye fathers and mothers, ye husbands and wives, ye fair ones, how is it that ye could have fallen! But behold, ye are gone, and my sorrows cannot bring your return."

Words, just words. I had read them numerous times, but until now I had not felt the power of the emotions and reality behind these words. They were like some forgotten memories that bubbled up to the surface as these words came alive before my eyes. His words became my memories of a nation once great and good, kind and gentle, a nation once filled with people willing to sacrifice their very lives for God and their fellow man. That nation now is but a withering shadow of its former self. Mormon lamented for a Nephite civilization whose beautiful cities once covered his homeland, and for a people who once were cultured and civilized. He must have felt the weight and sorrow that comes from watching those you love turn from righteousness to a life of evil, a life that you know will destroy them. For him, that sorrow was magnified millions of times, for those who died were not just words, they were people he knew. They were friends and associates. They were children playing in the streets and women in the markets. They were people he once greeted in business and in church. They were the workers in the shops and in the fields, the soldiers in the military and yes, they were his family. Then they were gone, consumed by the consequences of the evil that they embraced.

Words, just words that now have come alive as I look with sorrow over a modern nation in ruins, a nation once filled with people whom I loved, a nation once filled with people who had also embraced evil. That nation has now been consumed away by the consequences of that evil. The historical verity for the consequences of sin to repeat themselves shows no regard for time, geography, technology or wealth. Now I too stand as a witness to the truth that not just people but also nations are held accountable for their sins. It is as though the destruction of America was some kind of a delayed time broadcast of the Nephite nation's demise, a kind of instant rerun 1600 years later.

Words, just words that now have become a shared memory with that great prophet from so long ago. But there is a difference. For Mormon the end was the total loss of all he knew, and then silence for 1400 years. For me the result is different. For me, out of the "ashes" a nation of righteousness even now is rising around me in these mountains. This time there will be no silence, for there are yet millions who love the

Lord and are willing to serve Him. The tragedy is that their number represents such a small portion of what once was the United States of America.

Long ago DeTocqueville said that America was great because it was good, and so it was. Generally speaking, the golden threads of that goodness found themselves woven through the fabric of our country for several hundred years. Then some generations back, the arrogance of evil men began the systematic removal of that goodness and truth that had bound us together for so long. Strand by strand the strength of our national fabric was stripped bare, until the cloth that remained bore only the most superficial resemblance to its previous self. It had the appearance, but the substance was gone and so was its strength. Forgotten was the truth that strength and power are found in righteousness and a pure Christ-like love. Forgotten was the humble voice of gratitude from a once grateful nation that had looked to heaven for its guiding and protecting hand. Ignored were the words of almighty God who decreed that this land was a choice and a promised land, and that whatever nation should possess it must serve Christ or be swept off when they were ripe in iniquity. Ignored were the words of King Mosiah who warned that when the voice of the people would choose iniquity, they would be visited with great destruction.

Like the Nephites before us, we had become a perverse people, delighting in mischief, denying and rejecting the words of Christ, reveling in all manner of abominations, boasting in our own might and wealth, taking advantage of one another and running after violence and sin. Our people and leaders actually came to think that their wealth and power came from their own wisdom, their own business acumen, and from their huge military might and clever political intrigues. Now that has failed and the wicked are gone or dying, and I feel to say as Mormon said, "Oh ye fair ones, how could ye have departed from the ways of the Lord... Behold, if ye had not done this, ye would not have fallen. But behold, ye are fallen, and I mourn your loss." Words once ancient now are alive again, and all too real.

I am Clay Freeman. I have watched change after change wash over our country like successive tidal waves. Those changes have evolved from chaos, to tyranny, to war and invasion. Now, those destructive waters are receding.

The war is coming to an end. Soon the invaders will be gone, save those who begged to stay. Our reconnaissance is sending back sad but vivid pictures of a land filled with desolation. Each town they pass through, each city they explore is empty. The inhabitants are gone. The ferocious nature of the invasion is shown with each turn of the head. Bombed out buildings fill each city center. Block upon block of houses stand as forlorn witnesses of the cruel drama that had so recently been acted out on each street. Homes and businesses alike seem to mourn their masters, who once gave them life. Now they silently await an unknown future, their doors ajar and windows broken. Strewn about the streets and countryside are the decaying bodies of a once beautiful people, their fine and costly apparel now rent and stained. Everywhere, there are cars and trucks abandoned. The only things moving are the beasts of the forest, the roving packs of dogs and the fowls of the air. They have been feeding on the bodies of the dead. The stench of death wafts about, carried by the winds.

State by state, the reports indicate a startling fulfillment of the Lord's warning that all the evil people would be swept away in an overflowing scourge of destruction. Each search party is finding the same sad vista. Entire states now stand empty, devoid of human inhabitants. This same story is being found up and down the West Coast, throughout the Midwest and South, and along the East Coast. The stated purpose of the Alliance Army, which was to destroy the U.S. population, has been achieved with unimaginable completeness. Who would have thought that they could be that thorough? I will tell more later.

The great economic strength of our country now sits idle. The farmlands grow only wildflowers and grass. The factories are quiet, except for the buzzing of flies and the scurrying feet of mice. Shopping centers, convenience stores and malls bear mute witness to the wanton looting and vandalism that swept through them, only to leave them desolate and rejected once the mobs had what they wanted. The great investment houses, commodity markets and stock exchanges, all stand in startling silence, like ancient temples recently vacated by their disillusioned worshipers who suddenly realized that their gods were false. The once brilliant lights of the cities, that brightly flaunted their defiance against the night, are gone, revealing a glittering sky filled with stars. Power plants, great and small, no longer work, but seem to sit in fitful sleep awaiting someone to wake them. Everywhere, the promise of America seems in ruins. Only in the western mountains is that promise still shining, and it is getting brighter by the day.

Truly, America is a land of promise, established by the loving hand of an almighty God. He decreed that whosoever lived here must worship him in righteousness, and then he promised that if they would do this, he would bless them with freedom and prosperity. That freedom and prosperity was poured out in abundance upon the heads of our founding fathers. They had streamed across the Atlantic Ocean in search of religious and political freedom, and they found it. That freedom grew, fitfully at first, but then it began to coalesce into a need for independence that found its greatest bloom in the Constitution. The oppressive and paternalistic hand of government was finally gone. The full breath of freedom invigorated our infant nation and it flourished, both spiritually and physically, as our forefathers sought to follow Christ and make their own fortunes. The expediency of self-interest in a moral and self-reliant people created a panorama of prosperity that dazzled the eyes of people all over the world.

Then a change began. The seductive voices of self-appointed intellects began to disparage the political wisdom of our founding fathers and the divine wisdom of Christ. The oppressive and paternalistic hand of government again began to creep in, only now it was not coming from a monarchy in England, it was being fashioned right here in America, in our own halls of power and finance. Like some deadly virus that spreads ever so slowly at first, it grew. Each change was so small that surely no one would object, and, of course, each change was for our "good," and was done in the name of social justice and fairness. The philosophy of socialism and social psychology was the vehicle whereby evil men set themselves up as our leaders and caretakers.

Their arrogance knew no bounds, as they said they knew better than the average citizen of this country about how to run our economy, our government, our education system, our media and our homes.

These evil men hated the Constitution, for it hindered their grab for power, but they knew the people of America would not easily give it up. So, in the name of creating a "living" Constitution, these evil ones designed a way to "redefine" the Constitution. With lies and deceptions they cut one piece of truth after another out of the cloth our founding fathers had woven so carefully. The powers of the government were expanded ever so slowly, even as the liberties of the people were stolen away. Incrementalism, they called it. Do it in small bits, they said, and the people will accept it, never realizing where all these "little" changes were going. Vast tracts of land were put under government control. A central bank was created that was privately owned. A tax system was established that would allow for the confiscation of income to pay for the socialist programs. The government claimed the need to control the education system, so that a subtle propaganda program could be created that would turn our children away from the truths of the founding fathers and Christ, and lead them toward a humanistic and socialistic system. A need to remove Christ from government, education and public life would be falsely pushed on the public in the name of Thomas Jefferson. These evil men claimed the government had a responsibility to protect us at every turn, even as they increasingly interfered in our homes and families. They redefined what was good for our children, and callously destroyed many families who disagreed with them.

On and on these changes went until the philosophy of socialism and social psychology had contaminated every aspect of American life. Over time the public allowed itself to be seduced by the fervent but false promises of the paternalistic attitude of government, which claimed to serve all, but in reality only served itself. The more these leaders claimed to care about us and feel our pain, the more they used the masses to achieve their own goals, enslaving them in the process. Even as these evil ones drained the country of its wealth by excessive taxation, they threw some scraps back to the people. These scraps, however, were entangled with so many strings that the population of the country soon found itself tied in on every side with laws, regulations and bureaucrats. Soon the burden was so great that the back of the economy was broken. This catastrophe was greatly magnified by the spiritual bankruptcy of the country.

The people in this great land of promise now had broken the divine mandate that governs this continent. Generally, they were no longer righteous and were actively rejecting Christ and his commandments. Twice before, in past millennia, great civilizations had arisen on this land, only to turn to evil and finally be destroyed. There is a second part to God's promise for this chosen continent. It says that if the people should turn away from Christ, and become ripe in iniquity, they will be destroyed. God has decreed that no evil civilization would be allowed to continue here forever, and so it was, and so it is now. There is an allegory that perhaps expresses this more clearly.

ALLEGORY OF THE MANSION

There was a landlord who built a beautiful mansion on his choicest piece of land. Of all his properties it was the finest, and so he said, "I will save this mansion and land for my most faithful children." And he set up a strict and unbreakable lease with the property, that whosoever lived there must honor him and take care of the mansion and keep it in good repair, or they would be destroyed. So he sent some of his most faithful children to live there. He told them that they could live there as long as they obeyed the lease that he had set up with the property. For a long time they honored the lease and lived happily. Then they began to damage the mansion and left it in disrepair. The landlord sent some of his servants to warn his children that they must obey the lease or they would be destroyed. These rebellious children ignored his warnings and killed his servants. Soon they became angry one with another and divided into two groups, and ended up killing all within the mansion. This grieved the landlord, but he desired still the use of this choice place. So he cleansed and repaired the mansion, and sent others of his children to live at the property. They, too, were told of the strict and unbreakable lease. For a time, this second group of his children honored the lease and lived happily. Then they, too, began to damage the mansion and leave it in disrepair. So he sent some of his servants to warn this second group of children that they must obey the lease or something bad would occur, but these children also ignored his warnings, and killed his servants. Soon, they also divided into two groups and began fighting among themselves. In time, half of these children died from the fighting. This time, the landlord evicted the remaining half of his children from the mansion. He forced them to live in the shed behind the mansion where they suffered greatly. Now he said "these my faithful children have disregarded my choice property, so I will give it to strangers." So, for the second time, he cleansed and repaired his mansion. Then he sent for the strangers to come and live in the mansion. After a short time, the landlord called a third group of his faithful children from a far country to come and live in the mansion with the strangers. His children told the strangers of the landlord's lease, and admonished them to honor it. They told the strangers that the lease was strict and unbreakable. For a time, the strangers and this third group of his children, lived happily in the mansion. They obeyed the lease. Then some of the strangers began to damage the mansion and leave it in disrepair. They also invited foreigners in who knew not the landlord. In their pride, these strangers and foreigners now said to themselves, "we have not seen the landlord for a long time. Therefore, let us kill his children and take this choice property for ourselves." So they plotted. The landlord knew of their great evil, so he sent some of his servants to warn these people that they must obey the lease or they would be destroyed, but these evil ones ignored the warning and killed some of his servants. Sadly, half of the landlords children in the third group joined the evil men. Gladly, a small group of the strangers listened to the landlord's servants and repented and joined with the still faithful children of the landlord. Now for the third time, the inhabitants of the mansion were divided into two groups, a larger group plotting to seize the mansion, and a smaller group trying to honor the lease. At this time, the remnant of the landlord's children from the second group, who had been living in the shed, humbled themselves and asked the landlord to forgive them, and let them live in the mansion again. The landlord saw their humility, that it was genuine and permanent, and so he said, "Yes, you may live in the mansion again. But first, we must cleanse the mansion of all the evil strangers and foreigners who plot against me and my righteous children." The landlord waited until the evil ones began persecuting his righteous children. He knew this would strengthen his faithful children and reveal those who were not worthy of remaining in the mansion. At this point, before the plot of the evil ones could be fully carried out, the landlord called forth his many servants from a far and armed them with power. He also armed his righteous children in the mansion, and those in the shed, with power. Now his servants and righteous children came together. They destroyed the evil ones. Then the landlord burned the choice property to rid it of the corruption that the evil ones had caused, and he rebuilt his mansion and gave it over to his faithful children from the second and third groups, along with the few faithful strangers. They lived happily in the mansion.

As the allegory foretold, the wicked are almost gone in America. Righteousness has finally returned and is now found in every aspect of life, from our families, to our businesses, to our schools, to our churches, and finally to our government. Our prosperity has returned and soon we will go back and begin building the New Jerusalem. I look forward to seeing my children and grandchildren grow up and live in this new era. Things are becoming so good now that it is helping our memories and images of the recent destructions and sorrows to fade away. But I am getting ahead of myself. Let me go back and start from the beginning of the trouble, before the time of great sorrow gripped the nation.

CHAPTER 2

THE FOUNDATION

It was the beginning of the year of the collapse. On the surface it was a time of great prosperity. Business seemed healthy, the stock market was high, banks were lending and people were buying. The government said all was well in America, and indeed, so it seemed. Even the world agreed. But much of the rest of the world was experiencing stagnation or worse. In parts of Europe, Asia, and South America, their economies were in deep recession or outright depression, although few in the media would actually use that word. All eyes looked to America where the hoped-for engine of their recovery appeared to be humming along. Indeed we were heady with the power of our position, almost arrogant in the open accolades repeatedly heaped upon the United States: moral leader of the world, the only superpower, policeman of the world, the economic envy of the world, etc.

It is a curious characteristic of mankind that if an idea is repeated loud enough and often enough, people tend to believe it, whether or not it is true. In spite of much evidence to the contrary, we had been repeatedly told how great things were in America. We believed these claims. So it was that the general feeling across the country was one of confidence, a confidence that showed itself in a willingness to buy, a willingness to invest and a willingness to tolerate scandal. However, the beauty and strength of our position turned out to be more of a Trojan horse than a blessing, but few saw it at the time.

I was aware of the prophecies, visions, dreams, and warnings that God had given us through his scriptures, modern prophets, and leaders. I was aware of the ever-increasing volume of personal revelation and inspiration that was prompting people to accelerate their preparations for the prophesied changes. I knew that those changes were to be dramatic, difficult and even painful at times, as the world we lived in was cleansed and prepared for the marvelous Zion society that was to follow. Yet things had been good for so long, it was hard to imagine it changing anytime soon. I had a vested interest in the way things were. My business was going well and things seemed good for all around us. These prophecies seemed to apply to some distant time and place that would be for someone else, not me. Then that feeling started to change and cracks began to appear in the seemingly great structure of my world.

The cracks started about two years before the collapse. My wife, Anna, came to me with some concerns about the schools that our two younger children were attending. Kayla was in elementary school, and Deanna was in high school. The problems surfaced first with Kayla.

"Clay, I'm concerned that something is wrong at Kayla's school. Kayla is not learning as much as Robert did at her age, and I've been visiting the school to see why. Things have changed a lot from the past."

My reaction initially was that she was overreacting. I said, "maybe it's just Kayla. She might not be as talented at academics as Robert and Deanna are."

Her reaction was vehement and immediate, "No! That's not it at all! The way the school teaches and what they teach is different."

"Okay, okay! What is it that's happening?" I asked. I could tell when something was firmly set in her mind and thought out. I'd learned to trust her insights.

"Clay, a few years ago a new principal came to the school. She instituted a new education program. Almost immediately most of the old, faithful teachers, the good ones, left. They disagreed with her approach. At the time I thought it was an overreaction, but I see now that the new educational approach is very different from the old. The two approaches are not compatible."

Now I was curious. I asked, "What do you mean different?"

She said "let me explain, and this is just a thumbnail sketch of what is happening. The new teaching ideas are feelings based. The emphasis is around self-esteem for the kids, which sounded good up front, until I looked deeper. They are de-emphasizing grades, and genuine learning is sliding. Kayla is getting more teaching on social skills than basics. They are teaching her concepts like personal hygiene, which we give her at home, radical environmental ideas, which we disagree with, and tolerance for life-styles we strenuously object to."

I was amazed at what she said. "How do you know this?" I asked.

She told me "Clay, I've actually gone to the school and sat through days of instruction. I've seen this with my own eyes."

I wish this was all that was happening back then, but there was more, and it got worse. The more we looked into our educational and political structure, the more we realized that something was definitely wrong. Our government in Washington, D.C. and Salt Lake City was going the wrong direction. But, I get ahead of myself.

Shortly after the incident with Kayla, Deanna was given a test at her high school. It was to determine a career path for her, upon which her classes would be chosen. After the test, her counselor said she would be a great sales clerk. Deanna was not happy. She wanted to be a veterinarian, and the class track her counselor was suggesting would make it almost impossible for Deanna to get into a good university. Indeed, she would have to take a bunch of remediation courses to make up for what she would miss in high school. So my wife went to meet with the counselor.

"Good morning Mrs. Freeman. I'm glad you came to talk with me about Deanna's classes. We are excited about a new program that helps our students develop good job skills for their future," said the counselor.

Anna asked, "what new program?"

The counselor said, "the program is called School-to-Careers. This will help Deanna be ready for the workforce when she leaves school."

Anna said, "you are recommending training her for a sales clerk. Those classes are wholly inadequate to prepare her for college. She is more interested in being a veterinarian."

The counselor responded, "Well, I guess I can see if I can change some of her classes, but I'll need permission from the principal. We are just trying to help these kids get an early start on their careers, you know."

Then Anna asked, "but what if they change their minds later? They will not have the type of broad educational background that allows for a change. Besides, many young people do not make up their minds on their jobs until well after high school."

The counselor was getting uneasy. "Well, we aren't far enough into this program to solve that problem."

The more Anna talked to the counselor, the more restrictive the program became. It quickly became clear that this "help" for our kids would turn our high schools into vocational centers. We later realized that the legal focus of this program was to meet the needs of government and business, not the needs of our children. All the promises and claims to the contrary were just a sham. We wondered what was behind all this, the real motivation. We soon found out.

Upon further investigation it became apparent that all these changes were based on two federal laws that were passed back in 1994. They were called Goals 2000 and School-to-Work, which was called School-to-Careers in Utah. We wondered why, after two hundred years of unparalleled economic success in America without government help, our government leaders suddenly felt a need to guide our children's lives. We found their too-fervent concern for our well-being suspect. This proved to be prescient. These laws were hundreds of pages long, filled with platitudes, regulations and the creation of many new boards, which bypassed the elected will of the people. Anna and I read carefully through the laws. Contained within the numerous pages of these laws were huge grants of power that contained the seeds of the dictatorship we are now suffering from. These so-called education bills were really nothing more than the single largest concentration of political power in the history of the country.

Our federal and state leaders were diabolically clever. Who could possibly object to helping children? The evil within the laws was couched in terms of helping our kids and their futures.

A few examples from these Goals 2000 and School-to- Work laws that soon came back to bite us follow. Anna was the most diligent in scrutinizing these programs. She found many areas of concern. I will mention three of the worst.

First Area of Concern-all school boards had to comply with the dumbed-down curricula. If they did not, the governor had the power to dissolve the local school board and replace it with his own cronies who would enforce the program. We soon discovered that our own governor, right here in Utah, had pushed for changes in the law that determined who could run for the state school board. Only people he approved of could run, which meant that we no longer had a real election. No matter who we voted for, his puppets would win and enforce the federal program that was so harmful to our children. My wife and I quickly realized that in spite of our governor's claims to the contrary, he cared a great deal more about his power than he did about our children. As we studied these laws, we also realized that the same was true of our President in Washington, D.C. Such deception from people we trusted made us wonder where all this was going. It was like watching a storm building on the horizon.

Second Area of Concern-these programs required people to obtain certificates of mastery, which would only allow employment in particular fields. These certificates of mastery would replace the high school diplomas. The original diploma left the graduate with a wide-open field of choices for his future. That was to be no more with these certificates. To facilitate determining who could work in a particular field, the law provided for portable credentials to be given to each person. We knew immediately that such credentials would signal the end of a free and open choice of jobs for our children, and for adults who might wish to change jobs later. This became a major thrust of the oppression we are only now recovering from.

Third Area of Concern-last but not least, the law provided for the creation of 20 federal occupational-cluster boards. All similar occupations would be placed under a board that would eventually regulate the workplace. The boards would decide where we could work and whom a business could hire. They would give regulations telling the business how it must operate. A tax on business was even suggested to pay for the program. Essentially, all aspects of the economy would be controlled through these federal boards. No more free enterprise, as we know it. This was soon to be upon us.

So you see, the cracks in my world came from an area I assumed to be safe. Boy, was I wrong!

The next developments started swirling around my head way back in September and October of 1998. These developments made my world look like the House of Usher, which was finally to fall in October of the year of the collapse. Serious diseases of the human body often have substantial incubation periods, during which the individual appears quite healthy, unless a trained eye knows what to look for. A slight rash here or a few unnoticed pox there might be all the warning you get before the person suddenly ends up bedridden. So it was with the financial structure of the USA.

The first real "rash" that I noticed happened when the stock markets underwent large and serious corrections back in late 1998. Immediately government and financial leaders said it was okay, and the Federal Reserve dropped interest rates, several times, in a successful attempt to prevent a financial disaster. At this same time one of the numerous hedge funds that functions around the world got into trouble. This particular hedge fund was worth about a trillion dollars. In very simplified terms hedge funds depend on large amounts of leverage (read that as large borrowing) to turn a large profit even with small movements in the different markets of the world. However, if the markets go the "wrong' way for the hedge fund, they can lose vast sums of money very quickly and default (go bankrupt). When the markets were correcting, this hedge fund lost big, and was in financial trouble. There are many such hedge funds, and the total hedge fund exposure is in the many tens of trillions of dollars. For one to fail would jeopardize the financial structure of the entire world. Literally! For this reason, this hedge fund was bailed out within a few days by a group of central banks and other entities. They could not afford to allow the destruction of the confidence that held this huge house of cards together. The sad thing was, no one knew how much longer the financial gurus of the country and the world could hold the system together. The debt levels now obviously exceeded all capacity for the government to insure if it started to collapse in earnest.

This moderate financial rash opened my eyes to the precarious position I was in at my business, and with my house. The ability of people to buy what I sold was totally dependent on the flow of money, and that flow of money had come dangerously close to not flowing. This made me look harder at our money, the dollar. The dollar was not just for the USA. It was the reserve currency for much of the world, which made it exceptionally important. However, I discovered that the dollar was a fiat currency with nothing backing it except the faith of the people in the government and economy. It was little more than printed paper pumped out by the billions through the Federal Reserve, a private bank, and not a true government agency.

This system forced all transactions and property within the USA to be defined in terms of dollars, which the Federal Reserve released into the economy by banks, governments and people borrowing at interest. I discovered that this was a debt-based system of exchange. This system was basically flawed for two reasons that I could see. One, the money had no real backing in gold or silver. This left the money's value totally dependent on the perception of the people. This historically is a dangerous place for a currency to be founded. Anything that threatened confidence in the money or the government could destroy its value. Two, in a debt based system that injects dollars into the economy at interest, there are never enough dollars in the system to repay the interest. Let me give a simplified example. If one hundred dollars are printed and loaned at five-percent interest, then 105 dollars are needed to repay the debt, but only one hundred dollars are in the system. Therefore, repayment is impossible, unless the money supply and the economy continue to grow, with an ever-increasing debt. Thus it becomes apparent that a debt-driven economy must grow to service its interest obligations. In an economy as large as the United States, that interest portion was so huge that it amounted to many hundreds of billions of dollars. If that economy stalls or contracts for any reason, at the very minimum that interest debt cannot be repaid and will default. This does not even account for the increased financial damage that would result as people panic and stop spending the dollars they do have, thus multiplying the problem of repayment many times. So you see, a debt-based system contains within itself the seeds of it's own failure over time, since perpetual growth is historically not realistic.

It is important to note that even though the U.S. Federal Reserve System (Federal Reserve) was the primary force behind the monetary changes that were occurring, it did not work alone. It did its work in coordination with many other organizations, both governmental and private. For example, it worked with the U.S. Department of Treasury, as well as private banks and investment houses. As I refer to the Federal Reserve controlling the money supply, with all which that entailed, I will assume that you understand that these other agencies and organizations were intimately involved in that process. Therefore, I will not mention them every time.

As I look back now, I can see that the great prosperity of the time, and the repeated cries that all was well in America, were false. As we moved into the summer we had an economy that was quietly staggering under the weight of its own excess. It was poised to collapse at the first real challenge to the confidence of its people. We also had a social and political system that was rapidly consolidating power into fewer and fewer hands in preparation for a Caesar-like grab for power. One government program after another was spreading across the state and the nation.

To make matters worse, some members of the Church and some leaders were having trouble recognizing the dangers in the programs coming out of the governor's office, which the governor had received from Washington, D.C. These people even helped promote these government programs, which were little more than socialism dressed up as "love for your neighbor." The main problem was that these were government driven programs, not people centered acts of love. Russia and China provide examples of government-based compassion. It is nothing more than a trap poised to destroy all who take its bait. We soon saw such nice-sounding programs as "Baby Your Baby", "Success By Six", government preschools, "Justice Centers", and the School-To-Careers programs begin to destroy the very families they claimed to help. As time progressed, they became draconian tools in the hands of evil men and women. Repeated counsel from the Prophet to strengthen our families under the God given roles for father and mother had gotten lost in the rush to get "free" government help. Within only a few more months the price would prove to be tragically high and heartbreaking.

Outside the Church the situation was even worse. The country had spiritually bankrupted itself in a headlong race toward self-indulgence. People no longer accepted responsibility for their actions, and sought repeatedly to blame others for their troubles. Most people seemed caught up in the arrogance of self over all else. This showed in frequent abortions, high crime, violence, rampant promiscuity and divorce. The moral decline was staggering.

On top of all these developments, and probably in coordination with them, our country entered into a series of military entanglements. Back then these served to drain our defense readiness for our own land. Large amounts of hardware were used in Africa, the Middle East, and the Balkans. Our willing, eager acceptance of the mostly self-appointed position of "world policeman" was more than we could sustain. In hindsight I can see that while all these operations were going on, our enemies were watching with anticipation for the day when we would be too weak to repulse the attack and invasion that now covers so much of our once peaceful land. Those forays, especially in the

Balkans, served to drain our morale and hurt our will. In addition to that, demagogues in other lands used these events to stir up hatred toward the United States. That hatred later gave them justification, in their minds, for a war against us just at our weakest point.

The accumulated effect of these corrupt laws, financial problems, moral decline and military dissipation, caused the USA to truly resemble a house built upon the sand. It only waited for a "flood" to bring it down.

CHAPTER 3

THE FLOOD

Floods are usually preceded by a warning, even though it might be very brief. Perhaps there are heavy snows followed by a heat wave, or there are dark clouds followed by torrential rains. These types of events bring an awareness of the danger to come. It is at that moment when the realization dawns that the sunshine here will soon be obliterated by a coming storm with all its destructive force. That is how it was at the beginning of the year of the collapse. I felt we were standing in the sunshine of life, while a black storm rolled rapidly over the horizon toward us.

Things at home were great. My son Robert had just gone on a mission in March of that year. In spite of the problems with the schools, my daughters were doing well. Things at my business were going well. Inflation was low, and in fact, some of my supplies had actually dropped in price. Best of all Anna and I were getting along better than ever. We were doing more together, and were making a concerted effort to strengthen our family, as the prophet had counseled. Looking back, it seemed pretty rosy.

However, there was another side to this. It became clearer when I talked to a close friend named Alan. He had a large business selling heavy construction machinery. His products were almost exclusively American made, and they were selling briskly. But there was a problem.

"Alan, how are things going?" I asked. I had dropped by his place on my way around town.

He answered "Clay, things are booming. Still, it seems a struggle to stay ahead."

"What do you mean?" I asked.

"Well, even as my sales are going up, my profit margins are getting squeezed. The depression in Asia has dramatically forced prices of machinery down. In order to compete, I have to lower my prices as well. The problem is that my suppliers here in America have not lowered their costs enough to match my cuts." Alan was obviously perturbed as he said this.

"Can't you raise your prices at all?" I asked.

"Not if I want to sell anything. My customers will go to my competition if I can't offer the right price. Then there are the ever increasing regulations from the state and the federal bureaucrats. The cost of meeting these increasing regulations is rising continually. I actually had to borrow money from the bank last month to keep my cash flow moving enough to meet my payroll. I am hoping the situation gets better soon, or I'm not sure what will happen", he admitted.

I was concerned by what Alan had said. I decided to ask around and see if anyone else was having the same problems. I asked my brother Tim how his contracting business was doing. His comments were that the regulations were becoming so oppressive that his costs of doing business had been steadily rising for years. This was making it harder and harder for people to pay for the kind of construction he did. Lately, he had had some jobs fall through because the government regulations were forcing prices beyond what the market could bear. It was definitely getting harder to get bids to be accepted. As I talked to more and more businessmen, I soon realized that these two men were not the exception. They were very much the norm. As my grandmother used to say, "Something was definitely rotten in Denmark." Many businesses were quietly skating on thin ice and no one seemed to notice.

A similar problem was occurring with agriculture. Anna had a cousin named Billy. He was a farmer in Iowa and grew wheat and corn to sell. Many months ago the prices of commodities had dropped precipitously. He told us that demand for many of these commodities had dried up when the Asian crisis had started. From Thailand to Japan, those countries were buying less of everything. However, the cost of supplies was still up for everything. The years of easy worldwide credit had led to a boom in production capacity in almost all areas. Now, with demand down, Billy said the huge supply of worldwide commodities was forcing prices down. Even Canada was underselling American farmers.

Billy had borrowed some money several years back when times were better. He purchased more farm equipment with that money so he could grow more grains. Now, Billy could not get enough money from his entire crop, the larger volume notwithstanding, to meet his financial obligations. He had been able to roll the loan over, but if things did not improve, he said he might lose his farm to foreclosure.

This conversation occurred in the spring of the year, and Billy had that hope that we all need when we are waiting for things to get better. Nationwide, the spring rains had been good and it looked like there might be a bumper crop for Billy. He was counting on that so that he could meet his debts. As the country moved into summer, the rains stopped, or were sporadic at best. The crops that started so well were now languishing in the fields. Only those crops under irrigation did well. By fall it was obvious the harvest would be well below normal. My heart went out to Billy. I knew this meant great hardship for him, not to mention the thousands of other farmers across the land in his same circumstance. To make matters worse, our national leaders had been selling off America's once-huge food reserves. Where once we had sufficient reserves to get the USA through a bad harvest or two without much trouble, we now had only a month or so of food in reserve. That meant if our harvest failed we would be facing a famine for the first time in memory.

This was not the only development moving across the country that year. The political landscape was swinging more and more toward evil. Ideas once thought of as abominations had evolved through tolerance, until they now were so well accepted that our lawmakers at every level were writing laws to protect these evil ideas. In some cases people were being forced to pay for these evils and accept them. Each evil was masterfully disguised as something desirable, at least at first glance. If a trap is to work, the bait must be so compelling that the victim does not notice the deadly device upon which the bait rests.

So it was that most Americans at the time did not look any deeper than the noble sounding rhetoric they were being fed. If they had looked deeper they would have seen the dangers lurking there. Some of the dangers were:

First, diversity. What began as a celebration of the unique qualities of individual groups and/or minorities, ended up dividing the nation into multiple quarreling factions. The differences were emphasized so much that the importance of all we shared in common was lost. Before long we were not just Americans anymore, we were Hispanics, African-Americans, gays, whites, liberals, conservatives, etc.. This concept of "diversity" ended up destroying the very groups it was meant to help.

Second, consensus. Getting along, compromise, wow, it sounded good! All across the nation training groups were called to help people accept the new laws and regulations that were coming out. Remember Goals 2000 and School-to-Work? And what about helping people to be more accepting of homosexuality and abortion rights, to mention only a few? We were being trained every time we turned around, or so it seemed. But this training was not random, and the consensus was not spontaneous. There were facilitators at each session who "helped" us "dialogue to consensus". These individuals were carefully trained in how to get people to compromise on their basic principles. This created an internal conflict within the people at the sessions. That internal conflict would lead to the change in behavior that was desired by the facilitators' bosses. This was a wickedly brilliant psychological tool used to get people to back away from correct principles in the name of expediency. After all, who wanted to be guilty of preventing consensus? So change in the name of compromise, no matter how wrong, became expedient and common.

Third, homosexuality. What began as a plea for tolerance, ended up as a demand that we accept homosexuality as a normal way of life. Laws soon were instituted in isolated areas that defined gays as a minority group to be protected by anti-discrimination laws. Many businesses had to accept the homosexual lifestyle to the extent that they were required to treat same sex partners of employees like a spouse, with legal rights. Those who did not agree found themselves targets of harassment from radical gay activists. The costs legally and financially mounted rapidly.

Fourth, safety. The natural result of unbridled lust and selfishness was violence. The level of violence seemed to escalate steadily as spring moved toward the fall of the year. It took all forms, from increased road rage through shootings to bombings. The civility of the nation seemed to drain away before my eyes. With each new atrocity the cries to do something, anything, grew more vocal. In hindsight, it would have been important to notice that our state leaders and the president of the country were openly asking for increased police and military powers to protect us. At the same time these leaders were asking for more laws restricting or banning gun ownership. The public never stopped to realize that such gun controls would do little or nothing to keep weapons away from evil men. The only ones really affected were the law-abiding citizens, many of whom willingly gave up their weapons as the new laws on gun controls passed, both in Washington, D.C. and Salt Lake City. Indeed it was curious that the number of deaths from guns was minuscule compared to the deaths caused by cars, alcohol and tobacco. Yet no one seriously suggested banning these items.

When the founding fathers included the Second Amendment in the Constitution, the memory of oppression by England was fresh on their minds. The right of the citizens to bear arms was not about hunting. It was about our citizens having the right to defend themselves against any enemy, including our own government should it get out of hand someday. This truth was not lost on our leaders in Washington, D.C., although the public had forgotten. The imposition of martial law and dictatorship was now only months away. Taking guns away from the public was high on the list of priorities for the cadre of people who now saw absolute power within their grasp. The cries from our president, vice-president, the media, and our own leaders here in Utah, that our liberty and peace were at risk from radical elements was only a sham to cover their own grab for power. That grab occurred in the fall of that same year.

It turned out that the biggest threat to our liberty and safety came not from isolated incidences of violent radicals carrying guns and killing people at random. Rather it came from the organized, methodical imposition of martial law upon the USA, under the guise of protecting us from some danger. The danger did not even need to be real. As long as the perception of the general population believed it was real, it was enough. The "cause" could be a terrorist bombing, a nuclear or biological threat or chaos from an economic crisis. The end results would be the same. This time it was a combination of factors.

The pattern for dictatorship is predictable and repeated. It has been followed by peoples as diverse as the Jaredites and Nephites, Rome and Germany. America, too, fell into this trap. There must be an incremental but persistent concentration of power. Concurrent with that, the population in general must be made dependent on the generosity of the government. That is to say, there must be an ever-increasing expansion of benefits flowing from the government to the people, even as the people's ability to take care of themselves is drained away by heavy taxation. There must be a centralized control of education that turns the attitudes of the people away from God toward worldly thinking. Last but not least, the population must be disarmed in the name of safety. However, when only the police and military have weapons, then the only people who will be safe will be the ones who accept the beliefs of those who control the police and military. The above pattern has been repeated over and over throughout history as one nation after another has fallen to a dictatorship. Any nation that allows itself to be led by evil men, will always find itself with this same result. But let me get back to the story.

It was around the end of August, and the economic collapse was now only two months away. The stock market was still climbing, although it was getting more volatile by the day. It was experiencing wide and erratic swings. The bond market was not much better, and some Asian nations were quietly beginning to unload their U.S. Government bonds at every selling opportunity. As mentioned earlier, the grain harvest was not good, and our military actions overseas were not going well. Our own Air Force had even said publicly that it was concerned about its lack of readiness for any future action, especially to defend America proper. It had used so much of its weaponry that replacing it would take a longtime. This left us, as a country, with a window of vulnerability that would take years to fix. In addition, new gun laws were being passed that were getting a poor reception from much of the public. In fact the country seemed to be experiencing a kind of uneasy peace on all fronts. It was almost palpable that something was wrong.

Other countries now started dumping as many of their products as possible onto the American market in a desperate effort to keep their economies afloat. This began to force prices and wages down here at home, and led to calls for protective tariffs. A trade war seemed imminent.

At this time the president of the country went to Chicago for a series of political meetings. He badly needed to drum up support for his political agenda and for NATO. His ratings in the polls were slipping. The visit started OK. Then disaster struck! He was assassinated in a bombing attack at the location of one of his speeches. Many people died in the carnage, and chaos reigned. The vice-president immediately stepped forward and within a few hours was sworn in as the president of the country. A manhunt ensued that snared a group of self-proclaimed defenders of right. It is hard to imagine how such carnage could be described as a justifiable act. In reality it was anything but justifiable. It is an old cliché that two wrongs do not make a right, and certainly that was the case here.

The financial markets, already unsteady, were rocked by the assassination. Only repeated reassurances from the Federal Reserve, the Treasury, the new president and numerous other financial powerhouses finally calmed the situation. By mid September, all seemed as before, except now there seemed to be a proliferation of rumors about economic problems. The situation in China and Japan was deteriorating rapidly. Commodity prices were not recovering and a number of big companies were on the verge of bankruptcy. Right here in Utah it looked like some of the big mining and steel companies might close. Corporate profits in general were not doing well. Many companies even lost money. This news created a quandary, and the stock markets began to stall.

By early October, company after company was laying off workers by the tens of thousands. Unemployment figures started climbing rapidly. Construction at this point slowed down across the nation, and banks became reluctant to loan money for fear they might not be repaid. The availability of credit generally decreased. The Federal Reserve stepped forward and tried to loosen up the situation with lower interest rates, but was stopped when the dollar slipped a little against other currencies. The proverbial rock and hard place seemed to have arrived. Then an unanticipated wrench was thrown into the works. A series of private letters between a member of the Federal Reserve and an associate fell into the hands of the public. The letters were devastating. They painted a picture of the U.S. economy gone mad. The letters suggested that the public was irrational to the point of being manic about the stock markets, and that no stock position was safe! This was a death knell to all previous efforts to calm the economic seas. Confidence in the economy was lost and it was one series of falls after another. By now it was mid October.

The first dominoes to fall were the hedge funds. The stock markets dropped 1000 points within a week. Several very large hedge funds were hit badly and defaulted on their obligations. Bankrupt! The cry went out like a canon shot. Panic set in with other hedge funds. Attempts were made to raise the capital to stem the tide, but to no avail. The losses were in the trillions, and no central bank or private investment house felt it could take the risk. At the same time foreign investors, fearing their assets were not going to recover, started unloading stocks and bonds in voluminous amounts. Currency traders, or speculators might be the better word, smelling blood, started a run on the dollar. What had started as a trickle of selling only a few weeks before, suddenly was a flood. By the end of October all was in place for the collapse, which occurred on the last Friday of the month.

Across the USA, the markets opened to a barrage of sell orders. They all dropped rapidly and closed within a few hours. All the protective stops had been reached in record time. The sell orders were coming so fast that the brokerage houses and Internet trading services could not cope. Foreign investors were in a panic, dumping everything they had in a desperate bid to get something, anything, for their vast investments. The American public was doing the same. The huge stock market bubble had finally burst! Where there had been confidence, now there was panic. Where there had been hope, now there was fear. The Federal Reserve was at a loss as to what to do, and so did nothing for several days. Then it raised interest rates hoping to stop the collapse of the dollar, but it was of no avail.

By the Monday following, the stock markets of the entire world were falling; the U.S. markets all fell and closed very early, again at their limit. The cooling off strategy was not working. Everyone now seemed to want to sell. Every financial institution in the country was being hit. Their assets were losing value faster than they could cope. Banks, mutual funds, pension funds, insurance companies, brokerage houses, hedge funds, municipalities, state governments and the federal government were watching helplessly as their portfolios were evaporating before their eyes. The assets that were such a point of pride before, now were not sufficient to cover their debts. They knew that if this were not corrected immediately, a flood of bankruptcies would soon follow.

The political damage began streaming in as well. Cries for help, "do something, anything", were pouring in; but the president, the Congress, and state governors appeared as if frozen in place. They seemed to do little more than appeal for calm, asking people not to panic, but the public did not listen. Indeed, to the few who had eyes to see, many of these leaders were all too prepared for this crisis, and were soon to act with uncharacteristic swiftness, but not in the way we had hoped. The chain of events that had started building so long ago, and which had been accelerating for the last few years, finally came to fruition. At that point I realized that all those problems with corrupt laws, financial difficulties, moral decline and military dissipation, were no accident. The USA had been betrayed by the very people we had trusted to lead us, and lead us they had, like sheep to the slaughter.

In hindsight it was very apparent that this whole series of events was a coordinated action, intentionally guided by a secretive, international group of very wealthy men. Their purpose was to take away the freedom of all nations, and subvert the wealth and resources of those nations to their own personal desires. The USA had been the focus of their effort because of its great power and central position in finance. Looking back we realized that they had been playing us like a fiddle for more than 90 years.

It was their plan which gave us the Federal Reserve, which had such power over our economy, and which gave this hidden group of wealthy men a tiny portion of every dollar printed. The sums were astronomical, and we could now see that they had been systematically plundering the United States for years. It was their plan which gave us the IRS, that then took away our financial privacy and independence, and also served to finance the mammoth social programs that followed. It was their plan which fed us one social program after another, in the name of "helping" us, all the while our power was being drained into their hands by these laws and regulations. Social Security, welfare, education laws, environmental laws, OSHA, Department of Family Services, B L M, etc. None of this was really to help us, but rather meant to enslave us! And this it did. The tragedy was that the vast majority of people involved in these bureaucracies and departments were well meaning people who were totally unaware of the "big picture". They had no idea where all this was going or what the end result would be. Americans had swallowed the line of government compassion and help, hook, line and sinker.

As I see it now, so clearly in hindsight, we were as gullible of these evil men as Germany was to Hitler. Even as Hitler had promised so much to them, and then spread his tentacles over Germany back in the 1930s, so this secret group of wealthy men had spread their tentacles over America, and indeed the world. All this terrible suffering we have been going through was very much choreographed by them. The redeeming part to this whole tragedy was that when these evil men sprang their trap, it did not go as they expected. Oh, it started out as they expected, but then it blew up in their faces. The very people they had "spoiled" and been so "treacherous with," came back and destroyed them. Also, they had grossly underestimated the power of a solid core of righteous people dedicated to liberty. As it turned out, their very plan that was to give them power, actually served to concentrate and refine the defenders of liberty and righteousness, who have now reestablished the Constitution in its original form. Their evil plan served to accelerate the growth of the righteous government that is now replacing them. So we see that evil always contains within itself the seeds of its own destruction, and by so doing clears the way for its replacement. These same evil men had not counted on the direct intervention of Christ. That has now happened and has saved us from them. They thought that God had been silent for so long that they could accomplish this plan. They were certainly surprised.

The house upon the sand had now met its flood. It only remained for the natural consequences of all these events to unfold, which they did with great speed. It was like a high wall swelling out, whose breaking came suddenly at an instant. [Isaiah 30: 13.]

House Upon The Sand

CHAPTER 4

THE COLLAPSE

At first glance, one would not have expected a collapse of stock prices to affect the country as much as it did. After all, people still needed things. They still needed to buy food and clothing. They still needed to live somewhere. If they had a leaky pipe, it still needed to be fixed. If they were sick, they still needed to go to the doctor. As businesses met these needs, they still needed to buy more supplies to replace what they had sold. Trucks were still needed to move the products to the stores. Fuel was still needed to run the trucks and cars. Last but not least, manufacturing and raw material development was still needed to make the products the trucks haul. If all these things were the stuff of everyday life, then one would expect them to still work even if the stock market lost a large portion of its value. Yet, the affect of the collapse on our country was dramatic. The speed and magnitude of what occurred caught everyone off guard. It reached outward into every aspect of the U.S., like a giant tidal wave moving outward from a massive earthquake. It touched all our lives and the lives of people all over the globe.

We did not realize what an integral part of life the financial markets had become. Oh, I guess the thought had been expressed before, but the reality of this truth had not sunk in. The stock markets, along with all that went with them, had become the heartbeat of our economy. People saw the markets as a place to invest and place their retirement. They were seen as a place to make money for education. They were a place to raise capital for business. They were a storehouse of value and growth for banks, mutual funds, insurance companies, and much, much more. Even the rest of the world came to our markets as a safe haven for their wealth. Trade depended on it to a remarkable extent. The markets had grown so huge that the flow of capital was very much dependent on the good health of the markets. Without thinking about it, we had taken almost every aspect of our lives and tied them into the central financial markets of the country. The extent to which everything was tied together was so complete, that to move any part of the structure was to shake the whole thing.

Then there was that little issue of debt. Incredibly large amounts of borrowing had gone into building this financial house. The debt load of the private sector, business sector and the government, totaled into the many, many trillions of dollars. Dollars!! These were the same dollars, which were being pumped out by the Federal Reserve, at interest! More debt, and we must remember that the whole system depended on continual growth just to pay the interest, not counting the principle. So, we had a gargantuan series of financial markets that touched almost every aspect of our lives, and these markets were founded on a flow of capital that was debt-based on a financial theory that was flawed from its inception. The whole thing looked like a giant skyscraper with only crumbling stones for its foundation. It just could not last.

The reality was that America's financial well being, from our homes, to our businesses, to our retirements, to our government, were firmly tied to the health of the stock market. The psychology of the situation went well beyond this. People perceive their ability to buy the little extras - the bigger house or car, take that extra vacation or pick a nicer college for their children -based on how well their financial investments were doing. The flow of capital was very much dependent, in a real and a psychological sense, on the well being of the stock market and all it touched, including bonds and commodities. I started by saying, one would not have expected a collapse of stock prices to affect the country so greatly, but it did! For all these reasons, when the stock market collapsed, it had a massive effect, and the effect was immediate.

After that fateful Friday in October, the weekend news programs and commentaries were filled with talk of how this event was like the large "corrections" that had taken place before, one in late 1987 and one in the fall of 1998. They sang the song of confidence. "Invest for the long haul" they said, "buying opportunity" they said, but people were not convinced.

Monday began like all Mondays for us. We woke up, showered, dressed, ate breakfast and went to work or school. We were not big stockholders and so what was happening seemed academic and distant. Then I noticed that the day was not as busy as usual. I did not make the connection at first, but a few days of slow business opened my eyes. People just were not buying as much.

Anna was more attuned to current events than I and called around noon that Monday. "Clay, the markets are all closed. They have fallen to their allowed limit again, and the world markets everywhere are falling, too."

"What about the dollar?" I asked. Many of my business supplies came in from overseas, and a falling dollar meant higher prices for me.

"It is falling also," Anna replied. " It has lost five percent of its value just this morning, and there is more."

"More?" I asked.

"Japan and China have announced that they want their huge portfolios of U.S. government bonds to be collateralized by American property. They feel their good faith effort in buying our bonds should be guaranteed with public lands and real estate. They say we owe them that."

"Owe them that?"

That did not sound good. Wars have been fought over a lot less than this. Already we had months of hard feelings between our country and China and Russia over our forays into other lands. Our international "police" actions had done inestimable damage to the attitude of other countries toward the US.

As it turned out these countries were not interested at all in some legal ownership of American land. It was nothing more than a pretense of being offended. They were creating a growing list of offenses by the U.S. that they were feeding their people locally. These offenses would be the justification for their attack later. Anna had said for some time that she thought this was what was happening, and now even I could see the danger in the rhetoric that these countries were spewing. It is amazing how often such premonitions turn out to be correct. It was even more amazing that no one in Washington, D.C. seemed to catch it! It was as if they were blind to what was happening, as if all the prudent men were gone.

Mondays are bad, but this one had to be the worst of them all. As events unfolded, the whole week, then the month, then the entire next year seemed like one horrible, unending Monday. By the end of the first week, the dollar had fallen 20 percent against almost all major currencies. The stock market was down about 3000 points with no end in sight. The Federal Reserve now had raised interest rates again in an attempt to stabilize the dollar. But the dollar did not stabilize and the markets were hurt more by the action. Looking back, that first week in November should have been seen as a warning of what was coming.

That week was drawing to a close on a sour note, which became more dissonant on Friday, one week from the beginning of the collapse. I talked to Tim, my brother, early that morning.

"Clay, my retirement program for my business is about destroyed. I had it spread over several mutual funds, but they're not doing well" said Tim.

I was a little familiar with his program and knew it to be somewhat conservative, so I was puzzled. "Tim, what could be that bad? You sound very down."

"These funds each have a sizable stock position, and you can guess how that has gone this week. With the collapse of stock prices these funds have had a flood of requests from people wanting to cash out, before they lose any more money. Clay, the funds are having trouble raising the money needed to pay these requests. To raise the money, they are being forced to sell their equities into a falling market, which is leaving them grossly underfunded. They can't pay their debts or obligations" said Tim.

Now I was concerned because I did have a little money in a mutual fund. I had never given it much thought before because our mutual fund seemed to do well no matter what the economy was doing. Now it occurred to me that it may not be as safe as I had previously assumed. The noon news that day reported that many mutual funds were temporarily suspending redeeming cash-out requests. It was obvious that many of the funds were not going to make it at all. My fund was one of the ones that suspended all transactions with its members. Repeated calls by me to them elicited only dry statements about resolving the problems soon, when things calmed down. I realized then that a lot of financial institutions, mine included, were starting to default. That meant bankruptcy. My money was gone.

The same was happening to the banks and credit unions. Most held some stock position or were involved in those hedge funds. Many of these had been going under almost every day that week. They were a game for the rich, we thought, but by Friday the news services were saying that many banks and investment houses were being dragged down by these hedge funds. It turned out that many of these financial institutions were big players in these hedge funds. The first bank runs started in San Francisco, Chicago and New York. The week-long barrage of rising financial disasters finally startled people into the realization that their banks, especially the big ones, were very susceptible to this economic flu that was spreading. They could see that they might not get their money back if they did not act fast.

This "awakening" spread like a shock wave across the collective consciousness of the American public. By Friday word had spread that the banks might not be sound. The runs were massive. At first, only a few banks were hit. That was Thursday. These banks closed their doors and appealed to the FDIC and Federal Reserve for help. When word got around that banks were closing and depositors were not able to get their money, people actually skipped work on Friday to go to their banks and close their accounts. This happened almost simultaneously across the country. By noon the president declared a bank holiday. This was not received well. People were angry! They said the government cared more for the needs of the banks and the rich, than it did for the average Joe citizen. By Friday night localized riots started in some areas of the bigger cities.

These were the same areas that had been hardest hit by the escalating business layoffs across the country. Company after company was firing workers. The numbers were now into the millions of unemployed Americans. On top of the personal tragedy associated with the loss of one's job, the President had decreed that they could not get to their savings to help hold them over. They were livid and desperate! Many, in their desperation, turned to violence and looting. Somehow in their minds it seemed the thing to do. Parts of LA, Chicago, Detroit, New Orleans, Houston and New York were convulsed by this horrible unrest. The police moved in but were unable to quell the problem, and so by Saturday, the National Guard was called in. By Saturday night an uneasy "peace" was enforced over these cities. Other cities called out the National Guard preemptively to avoid riots. Many pundits were openly wondering how the use of so much force had become necessary in this great land in such a short period of time. Only eight days had passed since that fateful Friday. It seemed so recent and yet so far away.

What had started as a financial problem for the country had now taken on a decidedly human face. It was, after all, people who made economic interaction possible. These same people had an emotional side that could be triggered by extremes in circumstance, and we then had an extreme that pulled their trigger in a big way. They began to feel fear, and panic, and desperation. These feelings filled the hearts of the people across the country, and became an emotional flood that swept away the confidence upon which the structure of our lives was built.

On Sunday and Monday, union leaders across the country called for strikes to show solidarity for all those workers who were losing their jobs. The strikes and protests quickly turned violent as well. Their numbers had been swelled by people more interested in trouble than compromise. The uneasy quiet of the weekend exploded as more rioting broke out, only now the groups were bigger and the areas involved larger, and a new problem raised its ugly head.

Food shortages were occurring in all the affected large cities, especially on the coasts, such as California and the New York to

Washington D.C. corridor. Trucking companies had stopped shipping food into these areas, fearing for the safety of their truckers, their equipment and cargo. At the beginning of the riots, numerous trucks had been stopped, looted and burned. This fact was not lost on the truckers. Most stores only had a few days of food on their shelves, and this was not being replaced in these strife torn areas. Once again the National Guard was needed to suppress the riots, but the cost was high. Curfews were announced in the big cities by the governors of the states. They also imposed martial law in these cities and enforced it by shooting anyone found looting or rioting. Many people died; cries of outrage were voiced in the media, but to no avail.

This chaos was watched with fascinated horror by the rest of the country. There was an uneasiness everywhere, as if we were playing a giant game of Russian roulette, each area wondering when they would be hit. Then nature released her fury. A week and a half after the collapse, early Tuesday morning before sunrise, a terrible, prolonged earthquake hit the West. California, Nevada and Utah all were affected. Violent jolts ripped along the Wasatch Front in Utah, the Sierra Nevada Mountains of Nevada and the San Andreas Fault in California. The destruction was great. Many buildings were damaged beyond repair or had collapsed, with the loss of some lives. The road systems were disrupted, as overpasses fell and bridges broke into pieces. By mid-day Tuesday, the damage reports were pouring in and this was being hailed as the worst and most extensive earthquake in the history of the country. These extreme qualitative and quantitative adjectives were shortly to be eclipsed by a second earthquake two weeks later. November was not starting out well and it was downhill from there.

About two weeks later, in mid-November, on a Wednesday morning, again just before sunrise, a second earthquake hit. This one made the first one appear like an hors de oeuvre before a big meal. It affected much more of the country, extending from California and Oregon, through Utah and Missouri to the Carolinas. The motion was tremendous beyond anything I had thought possible. Our home was in a small town at the southern end of Utah Valley. Anna and I were awakened out of a dead sleep by a deep, menacing rumble emanating from the earth beneath our house. Instantly, the ground convulsed and everything was in violent motion for what seemed an eternity, though it was only a few minutes. The walls cracked, windows exploded and furniture moved about the room. Then pipes burst and I could hear wood creaking and snapping. I thought our roof was going to come down on us, but it did not. Finally, the motion subsided and Anna and I ran to check on Deanna and Kayla. They were okay except for a nasty gash on Kayla's head where the bookshelf by her bed had fallen on her. We cleaned her up and bandaged the wound shut with butterfly Band-Aids.

As we surveyed the damage, it was a wonder we were not hurt worse. I quickly turned off the water and gas to our house, and went to see how our neighbors were. Our street looked like a war zone. All the houses were damaged, and some were little more than piles of rubble. We knew our neighbors well and were relieved to see most of them come running out of their homes. We quickly organized and began a house to house search for those who had not yet appeared. At this same time, I gazed out over the valley below from a high spot on our street and surveyed the vast damage done. There were areas without light and other areas were on fire.

When Anna and I turned on our radio, we expected to hear of horrible damage, but were surprised by the horrifying announcement that some of the dams up in the mountains along the Wasatch Front had broken. Jordanelle was the first one near us that broke. Apparently, the earthquake had fractured the structure of the Jordanelle dam and the water pressure had pushed part of it out and then washed out the rest. Even as we listened, its water had already washed out the Deer Creek dam below it and was rushing down Provo Canyon producing an 80-foot wall of water. Emergency officials were desperately trying to warn everyone in its path to move to higher ground. By sunrise, the water had reached Utah Lake, and the flood swell was starting north into the Jordan River flood plane. Similar scenes of destruction had occurred all over Northern Utah.

Indeed, by Wednesday night, the full scope of the calamity began to unfold on the evening news. As bad as it was in Utah, other parts of the country had been hit worse. There were reports of vast uncontrolled fires burning in some of the cities of the land. Power outages and water shortages were everywhere and reports of more violence and looting were coming in.

This second earthquake almost seemed timed to hit the country in such a fashion as to magnify the country's financial and civil troubles in the worst possible way. That two week period between the first and second quakes had been rough. After the first quake, the Federal Emergency Management Administration [FEMA] had gone in to help the affected areas. The National Guard was already in place in many of the cities and insurance companies stepped in to help their customers. It quickly became apparent that the resources of these insurance companies would be stretched to the limit and they appealed for government help. However, the government was not able to do much for them, since it was almost impossible to sell any bonds at this time since tax revenues were way down. People were finding themselves in a position where they would have to depend on their own resources.

The country in general was not affected much by the first quake and at that time was still dealing with the ongoing financial and civil problems caused by the collapse of the stock markets. Commodity prices were still dropping for lack of demand. There just was not as much money floating around anymore, and people were jealously guarding what they had, using it only when necessary. Strikes were still going on around the country, but people in droves were willing to cross the picket lines in order to get work, any work. Within a relatively short time, we witnessed the collapse of the unions as the pleading cry for work drowned out the union's demands for solidarity.

Those businesses and corporations that were still afloat cut their wages dramatically as they struggled to keep their doors open. Prices fell at this time, too. However, this was not the end of trouble. There were still sporadic riots, violence and looting, but the firm hand of the National Guard had put a stop to most of it. To the world, the USA appeared to be a country teetering on the edge of chaos. This did not help our trade situation. The dollar was down 35% by the second quake, and all foreign goods were skyrocketing in price. As a result few in America were buying anything foreign made. This created hard feelings in countries around the world. They had been depending on us to buy their products to help them out of their financial problems. Now that help was gone. These countries had ignored much of our foreign meddling because of their need for our trade. With that trade now gone, bad feelings toward the United States mounted rapidly on all sides!

The only products that held their value were food and gold. Famine was stalking some of the large cities, and only the most forceful hand of the National Guard had kept it at bay by allowing some protected convoys of trucks to safely enter the beleaguered cities to deliver food. This shortage of so precious a commodity had caused people to be willing to pay almost any price in order to stave off starvation. It had even become necessary for many restaurants to place guards outside their places of business to protect their patrons as they ate.

Gold was another matter. The central banks of the world had been trying to talk the price of gold down for a very long time, claiming it no longer played a significant role as money or a medium of exchange. They had announced over and over that they were going to sell off large portions of their gold reserves. This was all done to keep gold down in price and off people's minds as a type of money. With this financial crisis and the collapse of the dollar, all gold sales by the central banks stopped as each one attempted to protect their separate national currencies. Talk began to surface of going back to a gold standard to stabilize the dollar. They also hoped this would stabilize the international monetary mess that the fiat money system had created. So, gold actually began to rise in value and was close to $400 an ounce before the second quake hit.

All of this had happened during that two week span between quake one and quake two. So one can imagine how the second earthquake affected this scene. The President of the country declared a general state of emergency with martial law, and greatly increased FEMA's powers. He set up a coordination system between the military and FEMA. He invoked numerous executive orders going back several decades that gave him incredible power over all aspects of our lives.

The insurance companies that had been struggling to cope with the first earthquake and their losses from the stock market collapse, now defaulted and closed their doors as a result of this second earthquake. They simply had exhausted all their resources and were bankrupt. The Federal Government stepped forward and said that it would help, but frankly had little to offer except military might. To make matters worse, the dollar fell again to 50% of its previous value in October. The Federal Reserve again raised interest rates several times in rapid succession to stop the fall of the dollar, again to no avail; it continued downward.

Across the country, there were numerous areas where the damage was so great that no effective transportation system was functioning at all. In many of the cities, the trucks could not get in, especially on the coasts. The train tracks were so badly damaged that the trains could no longer haul freight. The famine that had been stalking our cities so intently for the last few weeks, now pounced with a terrible ferocity. Like a tiger taking down its prey, there was no mercy shown. Large roving bands of hungry and desperate people now moved about, seizing whatever they could to eat, killing indiscriminately to satisfy their hunger. The tragedy was that their willingness to kill for food soon turned into a lust for blood. These roving mobs began killing anyone they could get their hands on, just for the "pleasure" of killing. Their lust for blood became so great that even the National Guard was no longer a deterrent to them. In some cases the size of these mobs was so large that the Guard units were afraid to confront them. Also, the mobs had armed themselves as they looted and killed, which made them much more dangerous.

The situation in Utah was a little better, but only somewhat. The strong presence of the Church here, with its powerful organization, had quickly stepped in to seek out anyone in need. Generally speaking, people helped one another greatly. There were areas of violence, but they were isolated and soon controlled. Transportation here was still functioning though sporadic; and some food could get through. Bishops of the Church used the storehouses of the Church to feed as many as they could, and asked each member to be aware of his neighbor's needs. This appeal to help one another was mostly heeded, and so famine was averted at that time in Utah.

Crews went about to repair homes and power and water lines, but it rapidly became apparent that this job would take a long, long time. One of the biggest problems confronted was the severe shortage of basic supplies. Even if there had been a surplus of money to buy things, the super efficient just-in-time purchasing method of American business had created a situation where there were no significant inventories of anything anywhere. Lumber, wire, piping, nails, etc., just were not to be had in the amounts needed. One would think this would have driven prices up, but that was not the case. People had so little to spend that the prices stayed down. The wage and price collapse that had already started a little while before continued unabated even as interest rates rose. In spite of all this, there was an unsteady calm over the Mountain West that made it a much better place to be than the big cities on the coasts. Even a few cities in the Midwest and the South were experiencing civil deterioration.

Now, it was our President's turn to show his true colors as he stepped forward to "help us". The collapse of the stock markets, the civil unrest, the earthquakes and the famine all had presented a reason for the Federal Government to impose martial law on a national scale. To the best of my ability, I will try to paint a picture of what that martial law looked like and how it grew. What started out as a bold plan to save us quickly turned into one of America's darkest hours.

CHAPTER 5

MARTIAL LAW

Only a few days after the second quake, it was Thanksgiving, a time to remember and count one's blessings. Oddly, where we were, the holiday was still pretty nice. Oh, things were still very bad, but people seemed to pull some hidden strength out of their hearts and made the holiday memorable. Our neighbors got together and we combined our food and resources and made a huge feast. There were many there with camping gear and some of the houses had stoves that worked off electricity. These still worked as electrical power was restored first. We obtained water, which had to be boiled and everyone pitched in and helped. The meal for Thanksgiving day was delicious and abundant, and it was a much needed break from the events of the past month. Better yet was the much-needed renewal of friendship and love that was to salve our souls at this time. We were starkly aware of the divine truth that man does not live by bread alone. We now fed our spirits on one another's love and friendship, and we feasted upon the words of Christ that gave us comfort and brought our remembrance back to Him who had given us all we had.

All across the West, neighborhoods and communities gathered together in similar groups to celebrate, and a great effort went out to see that none was excluded. In other parts of the country, some areas did the same kind of thing and the holiday was a welcome relief from suffering. However, the hardest hit cities were still racked by starvation, violence and roving mobs. On the day after Thanksgiving, Friday, the President announced on radio and TV (where they were working), that he had a plan to get the country back on track. He said he had toured many areas and knew first hand our pain and suffering. He invoked images of starving children and homeless families, desperate businesses and throngs of the unemployed. He spoke of the elderly abandoned and an economy on its knees. But he promised that this economy was not dead and would soon stand strong and firm again. He promised that there would be work again and food for all, and shelter for both mother and child, workers and the elderly. He was saying all the right things and pushing all the right buttons.

Then, and this was the part the nation should have noticed, he promised swift justice against anyone responsible for these tragedies and against anyone who threatened his efforts to put the nation back on track. There were a few who recognized the hidden danger in those words, but only a few. Very soon, those words came back to haunt us.

In brief, the President's plan laid out a series of changes that would be sweeping and dramatic. First, he called all our troops home from abroad. Only our Navy would maintain an international presence in the form of some ships on the high seas. There would be no more bases overseas. He said we needed to keep our money at home where it could do the most good. What he was really doing was bringing the military home to enforce his law on the nation.

He then invoked emergency powers granted to him by a long line of executive orders, dating back many decades. He also invoked powers granted to him by the Goals 2000 and School to Work laws. Anna and I knew what was in those laws. His words made our blood run cold. The President had carefully sought out a man skilled in organizing and planning. This man was one who was not bothered by the niceties of Constitutional Government. Rather, his background lent itself to authoritarian rule, which he adroitly put to good use in fulfilling the guidelines the President laid out for him. He was known as Mr. Edmunds, and so the plan was called the Edmunds Initiative. This Initiative was breathtaking in its boldness and sweeping it its scope. It was announced as follows.

The President would be the supreme head of this plan, with Mr. Edmunds at his right hand to administer and enforce the

Initiative. First, FEMA would be the administrative arm of the Initiative. Its powers were to be expanded in all areas to control all the bureaus, boards, committees, etc., that would be set up to operate the plan. This would be for the entire United States, at every level of civil government. It would have veto power over all elected bodies and administrators at a federal, state, county and city level. What FEMA said was to be the law.

Second, there would be a military man placed in authority over all military and police functions at a federal, state, county and city level. This man would use the military to create a military structure that would permeate the country from top to bottom, and would be the enforcement arm for FEMA. FEMA and the military would coordinate all of their actions under the guiding hand of the President and Mr. Edmunds. This ruling group, functioning through FEMA and the military, would become the chain of command for the country as this plan seized control of our lives, essentially turning the country into a military dictatorship operating under martial law. All people functioning in any position of authority in the military, the police organizations, the federal and the state bureaucracies had to ultimately be approved by this chain of command. Anyone not meeting those standards defined by martial law were to be released and disciplined.

All citizens were ordered to turn in their guns. Even weapons like rifles and collector's items were to be turned in. They said this would help control the rioting and violence. Instead, it was meant to prevent the public from resisting their takeover. A loyalty oath would be required at all levels to guard against "traitors."

A national identification system for all Americans would be set in place. They claimed it would allow for better security within the country during the time of crisis, and they said that it would also serve to make sure no one abused the many services this program was to offer. What they did not say was that it would allow them to round up all who disagreed with them and send them away. They also said that this new I.D. system would prevent hoarding and black market activities. They announced that this I.D. would be required for all employees in order to obtain work. A national employment bureau was to be established to administer this job distribution. Only "loyal" citizens could have work. All employers would need a martial law license to operate. All business would be required to hire only people with a national I.D. and an employment certificate. They said that a series of 20 national work cluster boards would be established to regulate all business. Ostensibly, this was to guarantee work for all citizens. All natural resources were to be placed under one of these boards to assure an even distribution of these resources across the nation. Especially, any food production and distribution was to be guided by one of these boards.

Hoarding was outlawed, and all citizens were ordered to turn in any food surpluses they had that exceeded a two-week supply. They said this would be used to help in fighting the famine in the big cities. In reality, they were soon to use this order to starve all who disagreed with them. In order to obtain any food, one would have to have one of the national I.D.'s. In addition, the powers of the Federal Communication Commission (FCC) would be expanded to regulate the content of all broadcasts, publications and public meetings. They said this was to insure that no one would be able to incite violence, terrorism or rebellion in the country. In reality, it was intended to censor free speech. They wanted to make sure that only their version of events got out.

They announced that there would be restrictions on travel between states and within states. They justified this by saying that it would stop the spread of violence across the country, and allow for control of scalpers and black market operators. They further stated that all able-bodied citizens, male or female, were to be productively involved in helping to get the economy back on track.

There was also to be a mandatory requirement for all citizens to "volunteer" to help build up and repair the damaged areas around them. This sounded remarkably close to involuntary servitude or slavery. They also said that the government would relocate people to different areas of the country, if it felt it had to, in order for them to have work. This relocating would not be voluntary, it would serve to meet manpower needs across the country. They placed education, at every level, under federal control. All citizens would be educated to be a productive part of the economy. Those who did not have sufficient skills at this time were to be re-educated, whether they were teens or adults. Work camps would be established in some areas to provide employment. Re-education camps were to be established for those who did not yet understand the importance of all citizens working together for the common good of America. Of course, the President would define what the common good was. To Anna and me, this was sounding like some kind of gulag straight out of Russia or China. We knew what dictators did with "work" camps and "re-education" camps. We soon found out that many, many of these camps had already been built years ago and had been held in reserve, waiting for this moment to fill them. Finally, it was announced that the financial system of the country was to be converted to an electronic system. All cash was to be turned in, and all transactions were to be by checks, credit cards or debit cards.

Taxes would automatically be withdrawn electronically from all wages. This was supposed to allow the federal and state governments to provide this "help." Bank transactions were to be limited in size, and approval would be necessary for anything out of the ordinary. This ostensibly would prevent criminal activity. This, in a nut shell, was the Initiative or Plan.

The President then went on to say that America had entered a new era of change. He said the wisdom of our Founding Fathers could not have anticipated our current crisis, and then said that this bold new Initiative was needed to save our citizens and our country. He appealed for calm and for our support and warned against all who would stand in the way of helping America fulfill its' destiny. He promised to do everything in his power to carry this plan out. He said that it would take a little time, but promised to move as swiftly as possible to get it going.

My wife and I could hardly believe our ears. We thought surely all Americans would see this for what it was, and many did. It was a politically motivated military coup led by our own president. However, the majority did not see this for what it was, but welcomed the "Edmunds Initiative" with open arms. To them this plan promised jobs, food, housing, and security. Through the years of abundance, unrestricted physical gratification, materialism and promiscuity, the population had grown so accustomed to compromising their principles that they had no principles left to stand on. In their desperate rush to get their evil, freewheeling way of life back, they were willing now to give up their freedom, not to some foreign power, but to power-hungry men and women whom we had put in place.

When it came time to lose our freedom, our liberty, it was not seized by some outside power or invading army, although there would be invading armies later. Rather, our liberties had been cleverly stolen away by our own leaders, right here at home. The demise of the USA was not an outside job at all, it really was very much an inside one! Like plucking feathers from some unsuspecting bird, one by one, our freedoms had been taken away. No one feather seemed so very important, until one fateful day, the bird realized it could not fly anymore. Then it was easy to cage the bird, and all was lost. So we, as Americans, had let our freedoms go, one here and another there, all in the name of a seemingly just cause. Each loss was justified as being for the common good. Tragically, very few realized that the common good required full freedom. Very few stopped to realize that the end result of a nation of citizens without full freedom would be slavery.

A nation cannot be free if its individual citizens are not free. By the same token, a man cannot be healthy if all his cells and organs are diseased. I looked over a historical landscape stretching back 90 years, and noticed how the once healthy body of America had withered piece by imperceptible piece. With each loss of a freedom, the believers in big government had promised more, and had given new regulations, laws and bureaucracies to "help" us. With each "help," we became more "protected" and weak. Now, with this crisis full upon us, the emasculated shells of our former proud citizens were easy prey for a demagogue offering a final government solution that would save us from ourselves. No, our freedoms were not taken away by an outside power. We willingly, even gladly threw them away for a mess of pottage at the hands of our trainers. Like dogs, most Americans groveled at the feet of their hoped-for saviors, even as the collar and leash were strapped around their necks. Only a few realized what was being lost and fought back.

After announcing this Initiative, our President first attempted to give an air of legitimacy to this take-over plan of his by appealing to Congress for an open-ended recognition and acceptance of all the elements of his plan. If he could get the House and the Senate to pass a series of bills encoding these sweeping programs into law, it would give the appearance of his programs being the will of the people. He also wanted this Initiative to appear constitutionally based. This would make it difficult for all those people and groups around the country who opposed the takeover to claim the moral high ground of being the defenders of the Constitution and liberty.

However, the Congress did not cooperate. There were powerful voices of reason who spoke eloquently against the Edmunds Initiative. They rightly described it as dictatorial and anathema to the liberty of the country. The House and the Senate in Washington, D.C. were racked by internal dissension, as they wrestled among themselves over what to do about the Initiative and the President. There were not enough votes to ratify the plan in any form, and there were not enough votes to strip the President of the powers so recklessly ceded to him through executive orders and laws previously passed, such as the School to Work and Goals 2000 laws. So, by default, the President still had his power, but not the legitimacy he sought. Repeated attempts, threats, and bribes by the President, Mr. Edmunds, and their staffs could not move the Congress to side with them.

By now it was the first week of December and all this political chaos was only serving to make matters worse in the United States. The stock markets fell further, and all around the world, the dollar dropped again, and the economy in general was worse than stagnant. Consumption fell again and more layoffs occurred.

This caused the rolls of unemployed to increase even more. By now, everyone knew someone who was unemployed. Feelings of frustration and desperation in these people were palpable. Most wanted to work. They had obligations to meet, debts that needed to be paid. Many had families with wives and children who needed shelter and food. To make matters worse, money was now so tight that tax revenues had slowed to a trickle and the Government was no longer able to raise the funds to cover programs like Welfare, Social Security, Medicare or payments to the American Indian Tribal groups around the country. Many millions of people were dependent upon these government checks to meet their daily needs, such as food and shelter. Now, most checks were not coming; the checks that did come were not being accepted by most banks. The attitude that they were entitled to this government help left many of these people mad, now that their help was gone.

By mid-December, civil unrest spread through all the large cities of the land as the mobs involved in the previous rioting suddenly found their rolls swelled even more by some of the angry people in these groups who once received government aid. The rioting became so bad in many cities that all forms of manufacturing and business ceased, as it was too dangerous to go to work. Even the very essential oil industry began to falter. Shipments of fuel became sporadic and many cities found themselves with severe shortages of gasoline, diesel and natural gas. Along with food shortages and famine, the country found itself with entire regions unable to heat their homes or operate their vehicles, and this in the dead of winter. It was like watching a giant snowball rolling forward, growing as it went. With each crisis, there were more businesses closing, which led to more unemployment, which led to more desperation and rioting, which led to more famine and suffering, which led to a greater crisis, which continued the snowball rolling even faster. So the situation grew in severity, sorrow and suffering. It seemed to be endless and hopeless. At the time, I wondered where it would all end.

As this circumstance continued its downward spiral, the President turned for the first time to the regular military for help in restoring order. He had already chosen General Stevenson, an army general, to head up the military portion of his Initiative. He was placed in charge of all military activity within the United States. Closing bases overseas was progressing rapidly and many troops were already on their way home, or soon would be. But there was a problem. Across the country, an influential minority of military leaders objected to the use of our military troops against our own citizens. These were honorable men who took their oath to uphold the Constitution seriously, and were not willing to violate that oath in the name of just "following orders." They knew that it was that kind of reasoning that had led to the horrible atrocities in Germany with its death camps in World War II. They knew that if our freedoms were to be preserved, they could not blindly follow an evil leader in the destruction of the Constitution, even if that evil leader was our own President turned dictator.

This internal conflict within the military leadership led to sporadic enforcement of General Stevenson's orders. However, there were military leaders willing to mobilize their units into action in their areas. As Christmas approached, many cities found themselves virtual prisoners to military governors who enforced the "peace" at gunpoint. Civilian mayors and councils were often reduced to meaningless puppet status and could do little more than rubber stamp the edicts of their military overlords. The vast coastal areas of the country, both east and west, were the first areas to fall under this dark cloud of oppression. At the same time, FEMA was moving rapidly to consolidate its control over all areas of the nation through the Initiative.

In other cities and areas of the country, the Edmunds Initiative was getting little support from either the military, the federal and state bureaucracies, or the elected officials. This was particularly true in the West, Midwest and parts of the South. Leaders in these areas were speaking openly of supporting and defending the Constitution. Some even accused the President of treason, and encouraged open rebellion against his grab for power. This was occurring even as mob violence, famine, and the economic collapse were spreading ever more widely across the country. The confusion, lack of unity and suffering caused by this internal political conflict served to magnify all of the previous problems that started at the end of October.

The most vocal voice for freedom came from our country's political conservatives and staunch followers of Jesus Christ, many of whom believed the Constitution was divinely inspired by God to man. Nowhere was this more acutely apparent than in the Mountain West. I was encouraged to hear the Prophet of the Church come out in open support of the Constitution. He called on us to stand up for the Constitution and all it represented, including contacting our elected leaders to let them know where we stood. He called on us to help our neighbors and to work together in each town, city, or neighborhood to see that none went without the necessities of life. All General Authorities, Stake Presidents and Bishops were called on to mobilize their members to do what could be done to help others, including non-members within their boundaries. He encouraged all members to pay their tithes and offerings that we might be able to continue to do the work of the Lord and be worthy of his continual blessings. He asked us to do all we could to be peacemakers and he asked us to steadfastly avoid involvement in any mob-like or destructive activities. He warned that no follower of Christ could promote violence against his neighbor. Above all, he taught us that the only sure way through the crisis we were in was in following Jesus Christ. He emphasized that our real defense and help was in righteousness, not in the arm of flesh. He also announced that all missionaries were being called home. The level of violence within the United States and Canada was making this necessary.

Throughout the west, a vocal groundswell of common citizens and leaders came together and called for support of the Constitution in its original form. This was hailed as a step in the right direction, and a series of petitions calling on the President to reconsider the Edmunds Initiative were sent to Washington, D.C. Other areas had groups who also spoke out for the Constitution, but none was so well organized as the western group. It was centered in Idaho, Utah, Wyoming, and

Arizona. It was significant that not all western leaders sided with the Constitutionalists.

Politically, many officials, especially at a state level had too much of a vested interest in seeing the federal programs continue as they were. They perceived their jobs as being on the line, and so were willing to consider following the President. Many of these people had long since compromised their principles to such a degree that it took only a small push to put them over the edge toward supporting a dictatorship, even though they refused to call it that.

When the President realized that his plan was not being universally accepted, and that many areas were openly defying it, he was incensed. He quickly realized that he could not pull off this takeover with the current group of leaders in the military, the police organizations, and the federal and state bureaucracies.

If the President was to succeed at this plan, he quickly needed to find people like himself to fill all facets of leadership at every level. These had to be people who craved power, were authoritarian and had a mean streak. He easily found them among the wide variety of people in our country.

Variety within the human family is almost endless, especially in a large population. Each person has a different combination of talents, inclinations, and desires. These combinations have only to await a circumstance ideally suited to that person to see him or her blossom to their full potential, for good or for ill. For some, there is a talent for leadership and public speaking, an inclination to do good and a desire to love, serve and help others. For others, there is a talent for leadership and public speaking, an inclination to do evil, and a desire to control others and to be cruel. Under normal circumstance, this latter group of people usually end up muddling through life hidden among the honorable military men, politicians, and business men of America. Often, they live out their desires in the good ole' boy networks of the states, counties and towns of our country. Now, national circumstance was right for the creation of a new group of men, like Stalin, Hitler, or Mao, and that is just what happened in the United States of America.

The imposition of martial law rapidly became onerous, and much resistance arose in all quarters across the country. The President was prepared for this. He and the cadre of evil men and women around him systematically set about removing from positions of power any and all who did not readily subscribe to the new Plan. It was truly amazing how easily and rapidly they were able to find people with the same degraded attitudes as themselves. It seemed that the evil within these people called out to one another, and they quickly elevated the power-hungry, greedy, mean, deceptive, and depraved people who surfaced around them to positions of power. They were equally swift in using their new dictatorial powers to fire, arrest, or kill all who were in their way. They instituted a ruthless purging process that began at the top and quickly cascaded downward and outward in a descending pyramid of terror. Each new level of evil leaders rapidly identified all opposition in the level below them, and "eliminated" those people. They then replaced them with evil people like themselves. This evil group in turn did the same to the level below them, and so it went.

This led to a startling and sickening transformation in the military, the police and the federal and state bureaucracies of the country. Where there had been at least some desire among the bureaucrats of America to serve and help the citizens they were hired to serve, there now was only a desire to serve our new dictator president and his minions, no matter what the cost. All concept of government of the people was lost as our government at all levels seemed to metamorphose into some alien monster bearing only the most superficial resemblance to our constitutional system given by our Founding Fathers.

This purge was instituted at Christmas time. While the country celebrated the birth of Jesus Christ, a ruthless removal of all people remotely suspected of disloyalty to the President began in Washington, D.C. New people were put in place with attitudes like the President. Judges were found who would issue arrest warrants against any leader opposing the Edmunds Initiative. Secret arrests were made and these people were locked away quickly and quietly, many just disappeared and were never seen again.

After the New Year break was over, the Congress returned. To their amazement, the Senators and Representatives found new people running all the federal departments in Washington. They also found that military units had been moved into place around the Capitol building. They were told it was to protect the Congress from rioters, but soon that proved not to be the case. A group of men led by Mr. Edmunds himself, came to the Congress and told them they were to ratify all the changes that had occurred over the Christmas break. It became clear that this was not a request. They were told that anyone not supporting the President's changes in removing all the disloyal traitors, would be considered disloyal themselves. The Senators and Representatives balked at this and called on the military to prevent these men from carrying out a military coup. At the same time, they called on the Supreme Court to rule against the Edmunds Initiative.

Word somehow got out to loyal troops that the Congress was in trouble. These troops moved into the city and confronted the troops surrounding the Capital building. Tense negotiations then occurred that stopped the President's men from arresting all the Representatives and Senators at that time. Intense talks ensued between the President and Congress in an attempt to resolve the impasse. In the meantime, the President had the Supreme Court placed under arrest and appointed nine new judges who were loyal to him. Word of this treachery leaked out quickly, and the Congress realized that it had no legal recourse to fall back on. At this point, the members of Congress realized that the best thing they could do would be to go back to their home districts and try to raise support against this President. Most arranged to slip away quietly, but a few stayed behind.

When Mr. Edmunds realized what had happened, he ordered his troops in, and they arrested the remaining Senators and Representatives. They were charged with treason. At this same time, all national press communications in Washington, New York, Atlanta and Los Angeles were placed under FEMA's control. The President then dissolved Congress using his power of executive order.

He then called a press conference with the new Press Corps. He indicated new elections would soon be held to call up a loyal Congress that would help protect the Republic. He told of disloyal congressional leaders, Senators and Representatives, who were plotting to overthrow our great government. He promised swift justice and said that anyone associated with this plot would be dealt with immediately. With the President's leaders now firmly in control in Washington, they next began purging all regional bureaucracies and military leaders in the same way they had done in Washington, D.C. Everyone suspected of disagreeing with the President was arrested and imprisoned or just disappeared. This occurred within a few weeks, and by the end of January many national and regional leaders of the military and bureaucracies were replaced by the President's minions. The leaders of FEMA and the military were almost all loyal to the President by this time. The national press spoke glowingly of the new leaders that were taking over the burden of governing our country during such a trying time. These same press people spoke of those disloyal traitors who sought to damage our "great" President's efforts to bring peace to our troubled country.

By now, the press was nothing more than an extension of the dictatorship. Censorship was everywhere, and the idea of a free press was slipping away rapidly. Only on a local and state level was there any criticism of what our federal leaders were doing, and that was getting more dangerous to do by the day. As we moved into February, the regional leaders of this martial law began aggressively arresting state leaders, where they could get away with it, whom they suspected might disagree with them. This proved to be much more difficult than the higher levels had been.

As I tell of the manner in which this dictatorship spread, it sounds like it was a smooth and easy transition, but that was not the case. Not everyone who disagreed with the President was arrested. Many saw what was happening and went into hiding.

An underground resistance quickly sprang up almost everywhere across the country. Some areas resisted the moves of the President so completely, that they went into open revolt and threw his people out. As far back as early January, many of the rank and file of the military, along with their local political leaders, declared they would take care of themselves. Even as the national and regional bureaucracies and military fell more and more under the power of the dictatorship, the individual states and cities were breaking apart. It soon became every state for itself, and indeed every city for itself.

At this time, the circumstance was one of financial ruin. The dollar by February, had lost 70% of its October value. The stock market was hovering around 2000 and all government bonds were considered to be almost worthless. Many of the big banks in the country were permanently closed and the ones that were open were foreclosing on property right and left. Millions of people had lost their homes and businesses, and starvation was everywhere. Mobs were the order of the day and only the most forceful imposition of order could obtain any peace, and this was done at a great loss of life. The only area with any degree of civility at all was in the West where the Church was strong. The strong cohesive bonds of faith still motivated many to endure these hardships, but even this was starting to fray.

Remember those citizens in the West who called for support of the Constitution in its original form? Remember that they sent petitions to Washington asking the President to reconsider the Edmunds Initiative. The President could now see that the real threat to his power was not in the fractured and divided states of the Midwest and South. He figured over time he could defeat these areas one by one with FEMA and that portion of the military that was still at his command. He already had the large coastal areas enough under his military control that he could deal with them at his pleasure. It was the West that was a threat. There was a group of well organized people there who stood firm for the Constitution. He knew that he would have to deal with them first. So it was that his plan for local control and suppression was first initiated to its fullest extent in the West.

Indeed, the President singled out the Church, to make an example of it by crushing it. His intent was that this was to stand as a warning to all other groups that might oppose him. He soon found that it was not that easy. The firm faith of a righteous people is a greater power than a multitude of greed and lust-inspired soldiers and bureaucrats. The light of the smallest candle is more powerful than the greatest darkness. In the same way, the persistent light of truth and freedom would prove more powerful than the greatest darkness of government control and oppression. This proved to be the case, although the battle was hotly contested.

CHAPTER 6

THE CLEANSING

With the national purge of the political and military structure of the country now accomplished, it was time for the President to make an example of his biggest and best-organized opponent. That was the Church. History and circumstance had placed the Church and its members in a position of great power and influence in the Mountain West. Huge portions of the population were members of the Church and filled many, if not most, of the political offices. Their firm faith in Jesus Christ and his prophet had led to a strongly unified population that had generally acted in concert on most issues. Indeed, Utah had once been known as a bastion of conservative thought. However, over the years, this had begun to erode. This erosion was mostly due to the wholesale absorption of almost every national program coming out of Washington DC, and was the handiwork of our own governor. He quietly and pointedly pushed each program, which the state legislature then passed into law. He was a master of telling people what they wanted to hear and then he would go and do as he pleased with little or no opposition. People just could not believe he would do anything bad. For years, the Governor's hollow claim of concern for us, and request for legislation to help us, were only fronts to increase his power. The President was well aware of our governor's duplicity, and felt this could be used to further the Initiative.

The President sent Mr. Edmunds himself to Utah, along with the appropriate national FEMA and national military leaders. Every significant local military leader was released and replaced with new military men sworn to uphold the President. The same occurred with every federal person of authority who did not immediately swear loyalty to the President. Even some federal judges were replaced. The people chosen as replacements in these purges were not just run-of-the-mill bad guys. These were the most ruthless people the President had available to him. If he were to make an example of Utah, he could not have squeamish people botching up his plans. This purge occurred in February, and by the end of the month all was in place for the next step.

At the beginning of March, the President's men moved loyal units of the military into Utah and placed them at strategic positions along the Wasatch Front. These men then went to the Governor and told him they were prepared to enforce the Edmunds Initiative upon the State of Utah by using military might. They also told him that he had better support the Initiative or else he would be replaced. There was no niceness in this. They were firm and to the point. They did offer a carrot, now that their stick was in place. They promised that this program would help all Utahns and would further the Governor's personal ambitions in the future; he was "persuaded." However, these promises turned out to be hollow. The Governor proved to be as pliable as they expected and bowed to their demands. He issued sweeping orders to all state, county, and city organizations that they were to follow all the provisions of the Initiative.

At the same time, Mr. Edmunds went to the leaders of the Church, and told them that they needed the Church's support for the Initiative, and said that this was the loyal thing to do. They also gave a veiled threat that if the Church did not cooperate, things would not go well for the Church or its leaders. The hope of these evil men was that the dual threat to the personal well being of the Church leaders and the threat to the Church as a whole would be motivation enough to bring them into line. Later on, they planned to put their own people into control of the Church. They truly had no concept of how the Church leaders were chosen or what caliber of men these leaders were. They grossly underestimated the Prophet and the apostles, and soon found out they could not be bought out or frightened into submission.

By the second week in March, edicts were emanating from the Governor's office in voluminous amounts. The National Guard of Utah was placed directly under the control of the new military leaders who had come into Utah. The Legislature was convened and told to ratify all the provisions of the Edmunds Initiative. It refused to do this and then, found itself racked with confusion about what it should do. Some called for censure of the Governor; others called for an order for all federal troops and officials to leave Utah; and still others called for submission to the federal edict in an attempt to save Utah from suffering at the hands of these military forces of the President. In the end, the federal overlords made the Governor dissolve the Legislature.

This incensed the citizens of the state and many National Guard units broke with the military and quietly set up a resistance to the growing dictatorship. Even some of the regular military men quietly supported this growing underground resistance. The Governor also ordered that all press, radio, and TV releases had to be approved before being given to the public. All citizens were told to turn in their guns, and that meant all guns of any type. All citizens were ordered to turn in their food supplies to the FEMA leaders. As citizens we were told it would be distributed back to us, that this would help avoid starvation. This turned out to be a lie. Only those who towed the line of the dictatorship would later be given any food. The rest were left to starve, even though it was their own food, given in good faith.

All people were told to register with the Utah Workforce Development Boards that were set up around the state. These were directed by FEMA through a state office. Employers were also told to register, ostensibly so that work could be distributed to all. Each citizen was told that he had to help and that public work programs would be selected for people to work on. They said that government identity cards would be issued through FEMA. All Utahns were to come to the FEMA offices that had been set up around the state, to register and receive these cards. These were to be shown before any government or private transaction could occur, such as doctor visits, school registration, food purchases, or business and work activities. The resistance to this was huge. This order was almost universally ignored in most rural areas, and on the Wasatch Front, compliance was spotty at best. At my work, I received a letter telling me to register my business, and my employees. I was instructed to keep a log of all transactions with any individual or company and record the government ID numbers. Anna and I discussed this. We were so repulsed by the unlawful usurpation of power that we decided to ignore this order, and to follow a tack of quiet civil disobedience. We talked to our neighbors and found that most of them felt the same way. This willful resistance and disobedience to these edicts was widespread. As the rope of suppression was tightened around us, the spirit of freedom grew in defiance.

The Governor also ordered his state school board to take control of all schools and see that only those things that supported the Edmunds Initiative were taught. This turned out to be difficult, since that would have required a major change in textbooks, manuals and teacher attitudes. Many teachers ignored the order outright, as did many administrators. FEMA, and the military, expected this overall resistance and had a backup plan of intimidation and fear ready. The sad thing was that there were many people in our state who jumped on their bandwagon and agreed to help carry out their evil work, even at the expense of their faith in Christ and his church.

There were many Utahns who had been amply blessed with life's abundance, who now found themselves with a vested interest in the things of the world. Even in this time of trial, they imagined that somehow they could keep things going their way, no matter what the cost or who might be hurt. They had placed their trust in the arm of flesh for many years. They had eaten at the table of power, of politics, of wealth, and of worldly praise and glory. They were well connected and had known how to use those connections. Now when a decision, a choice, had to be made, either to stand with Christ and all his truths, or to stand with the established bastions of worldly power that seemed so imminent, they turned to that place where their hearts had lain. They turned to that place where their desires, rewards, and efforts had been spent. People cannot serve two masters, and although they had functioned in both the Church and the world for most of their lives, they now had to choose.

Though they were "active" members of the Church, they had told themselves that religion and politics do not mix. They even said that they would leave their religion at the door when acting in public, political and business affairs, as if spiritual truths had no bearing on these areas. How cleverly Satan had deceived them, and how gently he had encircled them in his chains. Their repeated promise to "always remember Him" had somehow lost its meaning. These people did not realize, or had forgotten, that all truth fits together in every area, and that when the day comes that we understand fully all truth of religion, politics, science, and philosophy, they will be one and the same.

It was that same Christ who gave birth to this church who also gave birth to this nation. It was his guiding, protecting and inspiring hand that set us free from Britain and directed the creation of the Constitution. These people who claimed to love both the Constitution and Christ's church had forgotten that Christ was the head of both. Their now well established habit of excluding Him from their public, business and political affairs made them easy prey for Satan's henchmen. There are no places anywhere in all the universe or eternity where a power vacuum exists. If we do not serve Christ in all our affairs, in the end, we will serve Satan. There will be no in between. At this time of trial, these people had to choose. Their lifestyles and their very lives depended on it, and choose they did. Most had been committed for so long to the world, and the system within it that Satan had created, that they could not see their way free. They chose to support the Edmunds Initiative, even at the expense of the Church. That habit of leaving their "religion at the door," now found them moving their religion outside of their lives. Only a minority of the people realized what they had done and repented in time to pull their lives back to fully following Christ. They opened their eyes and realized that it was not the President and his initiative that was going to save them. It was Jesus Christ and his revealed word through his prophets and apostles that formed our road to deliverance and safety. It was righteousness and a closeness to the Holy Ghost that would allow for the personal inspiration and revelation that each individual would need to guide him through. Our salvation and help was in Christ, not in weapons or political intrigue. At this point in time, the truth of this soon fell upon us, as circumstance opened our eyes.

Compared to the rest of the nation, up until now, Utah had suffered only moderate pains from the financial, political and physical upheavals hitting the country. That now changed significantly. The order that had prevailed here began to break down as FEMA and the military moved to establish their grip on the state. Each program announced by the Governor was aggressively pushed, especially since these were really the President's programs after all. They knew that if they were to succeed with these changes in the people of this state, they would first have to break down their current way of thinking, trusting and acting. This would require great disruption. The plan of intimidation and fear was now unleashed.

For years our federal government had been gathering information on all levels on our citizens. The White House itself had purchased two Cray computers some years back. These were among the biggest computers available and had huge capacity. All types of information from across the nation had been put into them. Social security records, employment information, court records, military records, local school records, Department of Family and Social Services records, family information from programs like Baby Your Baby and Success by Six, gun registration records, and even food purchase information from those grocery savings cards ended up in these computers. Now this information was crunched and evaluated for any clues as to those people who might be a problem for the new government the President wanted to create. They zeroed in on Utah at this time. They identified all people who might pose a threat; the list was huge. They started out by going through state officers, and those on the list were released unless FEMA felt they could be used.

A massive media campaign began calling on all loyal Utahns to support the Edmunds Initiative as the Governor had instituted it. The media spoke of all the good it was doing. They even staged a few events to make it look good. They warned against people in our state who had tried to sabotage this work of salvation for our state and its people. They painted everyone who resisted, disobeyed, or fought against their work as traitors. They spoke of those who had not turned in their food supplies as hoarders who were selfish. They said these people were taking advantage of their neighbors in a time of great suffering. Of course, they did not mention that this food had been stored long before the crisis began. They railed against everyone who had a gun that had not been turned in. These people were accused of being radicals who cherished their guns more than the common good. They did not mention that the phrase "common good" was defined as everything that allowed the dictatorship to flourish unimpeded, no matter who it hurt.

A one-month amnesty was established during which people could submit to the orders without reprisal. They also called for a select group of loyal citizens to sign up with FEMA and the military. These "patriots" were to be inducted into a paramilitary force that would be used to search out all who violated the law of the land. These groups of men, mostly younger, were little more than organized thugs carrying badges. They had received official permission to terrorize and/or kill all who did not follow the official line. They were called The People's Defense Force (PDF). It was reminiscent of the cultural revolution in China. These evil leaders figured that if it had worked in China, it should work here. FEMA began training these people immediately and armed them with guns. Very soon, this proved to be the cause of much bloodshed, as many gunfights broke out throughout the extended metropolitan areas of Salt Lake City. The men of the People's Defense Force soon were infamous for their brutality, greed and corruption. They spread fear wherever they went. Entire neighborhoods became armed camps in an attempt to protect themselves from the PDF.

Where my family lived, this was not as bad. People here were more cohesive in belief and were more committed to helping one another. The attempts of FEMA and the military to make inroads here had not been very strong yet. They were still concentrating on the large population centers to the north. They figured that once the Ogden-Salt Lake City-Provo corridor was under their control they could get the rest of the state later. That proved to be a fatal miscalculation on their part.

During this time, the initial overtures to the Church by Mr. Edmunds and his people were largely rebuffed. Our prophet sent repeated appeals to the Governor encouraging him to stand firm for liberty, but to no avail. The dye was cast. Official letters were sent to all Church units in the Mountain West admonishing calm and discouraging any armed or violent activities in response to the evil that was occurring. We were encouraged again to use all peaceful means available to protect the Constitution and maintain our liberty. We were also reminded of the omnipotent hand of Almighty God that had preserved us so many times in the past; we were asked to fast and pray for help and guidance. Right after this letter went out, the Church instituted a series of legal actions in an attempt to get the courts to protect the Constitution, and enforce its provisions by voiding the Edmunds Initiative. It was soon apparent that all our new judges were in the President's pocket, and were not going to give us justice. Even the state courts were of little use.

Among the members in general, grumbling began to surface. There is nothing like a crisis to bring our true colors to the surface. If there is any inclination to criticize the Brethren, or to be wishy washy on the doctrine, it will show up in a crisis. Conversely, those who have hearts and spirits that are pure, and who are courageous for Christ, will shine more clearly as the spirit of contention builds around them. We saw many who now criticized the Prophet openly, wondering out loud why he had not received revelation earlier warning of this crisis. They said if indeed he was a prophet, he would have given us advice about the Stock Market, about our businesses and about our homes that would have helped us avoid the crash of the previous October.

Accusations of "false prophets," and "fallen prophet" began to surface even in church meetings. We now saw a sizable chunk of the membership began to waver in their faith. It seemed their ability to be strong spiritually was tied directly to the comfort level of their lives. As we saw an increase in the trouble they had in their businesses, homes and finances we also saw an increase in the trouble they had spiritually. Up until now, their "lamps" had looked pretty good, but it turned out that there was no oil in them. Now, when they needed the Holy Spirit most, they had little of his influence in their lives.

It is somewhat normal for the natural man to look for someone to blame when things do not go well in their lives. These people had bouts of convenient memory. They remembered those things which salved their conscience, and "forgot" those things which reminded them of their own failures and mistakes. They forgot that, for many years, the prophets had been admonishing them to get out of debt. They forgot that, for many years, the prophets had been admonishing them to get a year's supply of food. They forgot that, for many years, the prophets had admonished each family to be wise in their financial affairs so that we might be self-sufficient. Now with our financial and political house coming down around our heads, a scapegoat was needed, and they blamed the Prophet and the apostles.

Not all members acted in this fashion. Another sizable chunk of the members were faithful and strong. These members remembered the words of the prophets, and had their feet firmly planted in the doctrines of the Church. They accepted responsibility for their own actions, and were spending their energies trying to handle their own circumstances. These people were close to the Holy Spirit and were receiving inspiration about what to do, and they were drawing ever closer to Christ. Their "lamps" truly were full of oil, which now burned with an ever increasing brightness. The prophet Joel prophesied that in the latter days, visions and dreams would become more common, and indeed that was happening as these gifts were poured out upon the righteous to help guide them through the difficulties around them.

With this growing division within the ranks of the Church, we saw the beginning of the fulfillment of the words of the Lord to Joseph Smith and Wilford Woodruff. Elder Woodruff had been told that the Lord would cause a separation in the people and would cleanse his church. It was interesting that Satan's minions so unwittingly aided this process. As this dissension arose in the Church, Mr. Edmunds' men were thrilled, and thought they saw success coming from their plan. They had no idea that this would all turn back upon their own heads someday. Their inability to see the weakness of their own position was firmly rooted in the web of lies upon which their lives were hung.

Evil people by their very nature are blind, not because they cannot see, but rather because they refuse to see. They place upon themselves a set of restrictions that render them incapable of seeing any other viewpoint than the one that justifies their evil. As a result, they create a system of knowledge which they mistake for truth. This system of knowledge is so subtly and insidiously suffused with errors that it can succeed in deluding even the most educated people into thinking that their knowledge system is "scientific." The assumptions upon which this "science" is based are a mixture of truth and error and are essential to this lifestyle of evil. Because the foundation assumptions of this system are partly false, they will lead to false conclusions. As these people build outward on these false assumptions, they will create theories and beliefs which are evermore contaminated with error. Each new contaminated theory and belief becomes the foundation for more theories and beliefs, which inexorably ripple outward in a distorted expansion of every-increasing falsehoods, lies and deceptions. A few small false assumptions at the beginning lead to an ever wider divergence from truth; like two lines starting at the same point that initially diverge only a little, but over time the distance between the lines gets greater and greater, until finally they are worlds apart.

Let me give an example. If you assume that only that which you can physically see or measure is true, then by definition you eliminate all spiritual experiences and truth. Based on these self-imposed restrictions of physical evidence, you might then falsely conclude that there is no God. Based on that erroneous conclusion, you then might conclude that if there is no God, there then cannot be any divine law of right and wrong, i.e. no Ten Commandments. You then would erroneously conclude that each man is on his own to do what he can get away with since, without divine law, there is no reasonable way to conclude that there is any right or wrong. It becomes the survival of the fittest, the law of the jungle. This leads to the false assumption that man's existence is accidental, and that man might be viewed as the highest form of an accidental evolutionary system. This then invites the conclusion that man is his own guide through eternity, and as such, man's false science then becomes his god. So we arrive at a point where the powerful, the wealthy and the educated of the world often end up assuming that they, because of their worldly acumen, are better than those around them. Therefore, they feel they can do as they please, no matter how bad it is for other individuals, if they claim it is for the good of mankind. In reality, they are only doing what is for their own good, no matter who they hurt.

So you see, people can start out with a few small, erroneous ideas, and if they are left unchecked and unchallenged, over time they will blindly expand their errors until they do great evil, all in the name of "truth." The tragedy is that they soon get so caught up in their expanding evil that they cannot even see where they are wrong, because they simply refuse to see. This is what happened all over the United States and was then happening in a big way in Utah. Expanding circles of error and falsehood had been growing for so many decades in almost every part of our society that now the darkness of evil shrouded our country from coast to coast like some suffocating plague. It had infiltrated everything from government to business to education to the media and even some religions. Because of this, basic political and religious truths that were once universally accepted, were now universally rejected. Only a few groups remembered these truths and still held them inviolate. The largest solidly organized concentration of these people was found in the Mountain West among the members of the Church, and among righteous gentiles of like mind.

71

As for the evil people leading the Initiative, they blindly groped forward, falsely assuming that all would go well. They did not realize that their lives, efforts and plans were all based on a rotting foundation; a foundation so thoroughly riddled with lies that it could not endure.

At this time the Governor's leaders, along with the FEMA and the military leaders, singled out the local leaders of the Church, the bishops and stake presidents, and approached each one individually. They intentionally bypassed most of the General Authorities of the Church. They brought great pressure to bear on these local leaders, and made the point very clear that if the stakes and wards did not comply with their program, the Church would be destroyed. They also told these local leaders that if they would cooperate, guarantees would be made that the food they collected would be used to feed their members. They also promised to protect the members after their guns were turned in. Many of these local church leaders felt like they had no choice but to comply; they actually believed that these political threats might come true, and felt they could trust the promises of the FEMA people.

This resulted in some bishops and stake presidents asking their members to follow the Edmunds Initiative. They asked their members to turn in their food and guns. These requests were made of the members based on the promises given by the government. They were to find out later that such promises were seldom kept. One of the reassuring things was that many of the local leaders did not fall for the threats and empty promises of the government, though some did. The members in those areas where their church leaders asked them to turn in their food and guns, generally complied. This turned out to be a great tragedy. The already big crisis in the country was now growing in Utah and it was getting worse almost by the day. This financial and political crisis was now becoming a full-blown crisis of faith for many saints.

This crisis of faith, which now fell upon the Church, followed an all-too-familiar pattern. Several times in the distant past, a crisis had flushed out those members whose loyalties had gradually been corrupted by pride, worldly desires and political expediency. It happened in Kirtland as a financial crisis turned many against the Prophet Joseph Smith. It happened in Far West as some local church members and leaders colluded with the local political and military leaders to betray the Prophet, only to have those promises broken. It also occurred in the Sanhedrin whose religious, political and financial acumen became the poison that turned their hearts to treachery against the Savior. And now that poison was expressed in the willing collusion of some Church members and leaders who eagerly turned to the state and federal government which they had grown dependent upon, to lead them out of the chaos. In reality, they should have turned to the Lord through his anointed Prophet for guidance. Like Far West, agreements were made that were never kept by the government, even after trusting members of the Church followed their local leaders' advice in the areas involved. Incredible hardship followed that dwarfed even the horrible suffering in Missouri.

As we moved through March and April, the situation in Utah was severe. The plan of the dictatorship appeared to be gaining ground and the oppression was palpable. During this time the unthinkable happened. A few of the General Authorities met secretly with the leaders of the Initiative; i.e. FEMA and the military. They said they just wanted to work something out that would stop the suffering and save the Church. They had lost their vision of who truly led the Church. They had forgotten that all things are possible unto the Lord. If we would trust in him, He would guide us through this. Those members who were already grumbling quickly rallied around these men. The Prophet tried in vain to persuade them to wait upon the Lord and trust in Him. The apostate attitude of this group of leaders only grew worse. By April conference, the President of the Church found it necessary to release these men and call new ones into their places. For the first time in memory, there were dissenting voices during the sustaining vote. However, these represented a small minority. The majority sustained the Prophet, but much damage had been done by these apostate leaders and members. As is always the case, the greatest harm done by these men proved to be to themselves and those who followed them. Their claims of concern for the welfare of the Church were uninspired and hollow.

All members who had mistakenly heeded the call to turn in their food and guns, now found themselves on the verge of starvation and were virtually helpless before the oppressors. When they went to the FEMA aid centers for the promised food they were told that they must first make a loyalty oath to the President of the country, placing the President above all else; including family, church and God. They also were told they would have to receive a national identity card verifying their loyalty. In desperation, many took the oath and sold their souls, as it were, for food. Many others refused and found themselves being denied access to their own food. Worse than that, they now had been identified by the regime as dangerous, and found themselves targets of visits by the People's Defense Force. With no food or guns, they had to run, hoping to find sympathetic friends to hide them. There was a growing underground that did just that. Not everyone followed the Prophet's advice to avoid violence either. By May of that year, coordinated guerrilla attacks began against many state, federal and military installations. Bombings became frequent at these government centers and it was surprising how much military weaponry disappeared, only to end up in the hands of the rebels. There were yet many in the military who were secretly sympathetic to the rebels.

The Prophet at that time called upon us all to recommit ourselves to Jesus Christ and accept his divine will. We were encouraged to follow the admonition of Christ to feed the hungry, clothe the naked and give shelter to the homeless. By then, these were pressing issues as the government leaders and forces tightened their rope around us.

These government leaders were anxiously cultivating the support of the apostate leaders and members, even going so far as to broadcast their apostate views on the controlled media. They attempted to place those apostates in control of the Church's property, but failed. It was by then the official position of the government to persecute all active members of the Church. Anyone who showed loyalty to the Prophet was criticized as dangerous, selfish and subversive. The propaganda of the government encouraged all "loyal" citizens to turn in their neighbors for obstructing the efforts of the government. That whole structure looked more and more like something out of Russia or China. It became worse by the day. It was sad that we had allowed the power to do this great evil to accumulate in the President's hands; and this by virtue of the numerous executive orders and voluminous laws that had been so methodically passed by our Congress in Washington over the years. These laws and executive orders should have been repealed long ago, but were not.

Some months back, the missionaries had all been called home. That was actually a great comfort to Anna and me. We were glad to have our own son home during this terrible crisis. I am sure that most other families felt the same way. The legions of returned missionaries who had been coming home for years, now was augmented by this final core of young men who, for the most part, stood firm for Christ. The total number of faithful men was great, and that did not include the women and children.

It was amazing that all these changes had occurred within a short eight month period. Now the Lord revealed a number of things to the Church through the Prophet. Directions were given for the Saints to gather to specific areas of safety. These became cities of refuge where all who were in need were welcome. The only requirement was that they must follow the laws and commandments that governed our society. These laws were God-given, and the Edmunds Initiative was declared void in all of these areas.

At this same time, Christ began the establishment of His political kingdom on earth. He was recognized as the king, judge and lawgiver over all the earth. A council was started that would eventually govern all the earth under His direction. A series of basic laws were given, by Him, that became the framework upon which our political interactions were based. This basic framework would become the standard for all governments upon the earth. An announcement was made to that effect and all governments were told that He, whose right it was to reign, was now exercising that right. All laws, regulations, edicts and orders that went contrary to Christ's law were declared void, and each government was instructed to bring its laws into compliance with the divine law. The world initially ignored this call, claiming the Mormons were just a bunch of radial zealots blowing hot air. They said we would soon be put in our place. They did not realize the reality of Christ's leadership. Like a small seed that germinates in good soil and then over time, grows into a mighty tree, Christ's kingdom germinated in the soil of a Zion people, a covenant people, and began to grow. At first the infant kingdom did not appear very impressive, but soon it was to become as terrible to the wicked as an army with banners.

At that time, many of the Saints began moving to those cities and places of refuge. A great consecration of our possessions was needed, and it was willingly given by many to make this happen. All this work was done in good order, with careful planning taking place. It would take many months to accomplish. The Lord also said that all who wished to go to the places of refuge were to be helped. No one was to be left behind. Those places of safety in North America were designated all over the Mountain West in a corridor that stretched from Canada on the north, to Mexico on the south. Most of those locations were somewhat remote or protected by mountains, rivers or canyons. As we moved into these refuges, we were amazed to find that a few of the Indian tribes in North America already knew about these places. They had been waiting for this time of trial to build these cities. We worked side by side, and hand in hand with them in the construction of some of these places of safety. Some of the men of the Church were organized into units that served to protect the righteous as they moved toward these areas. Outside of the Mountain West, others, not all of our faith, heard of these places and began a migration westward in a desperate hope to find peace.

Christ instructed that righteous Priesthood holders were to be placed as guardians around these areas. All strategic passes and roads were to be watched, and those connected with the President and his government were not allowed to pass. This Priesthood proved to be so powerful that Mr. Edmunds, FEMA, and the military leaders could not get past them. Increasing areas of the Mountain West began to fall under the control of Christ's government. Those places Mr. Edmunds thought he would take later, were now slipping out of his reach. Mr. Edmunds found he now controlled only the large cities and a few of the smaller ones. This caused great frustration and anger.

Back in Washington DC, the President heard of these events. He flew into a rage. By now it was the beginning of summer and things were not going quite as he had planned. He was gaining ground around the rest of the country, but he had expected that. It was the West where he had hoped to crush his greatest opponents first and that was not going well. There were many among the national military and state leaders in Utah who were secretly undermining his work. The identity card system was not working well either. It was too easy to counterfeit or get around. He ordered that all "loyal" citizens receive an identity chip in their hands that would be injected under the skin. This was almost impossible to counterfeit and could be read by a hand-held scanner. He ordered that a round-up was to commence of all who refused the chip. They were to be sent to camps where they would be re-educated, forced to work, and ultimately killed.

The secretive international group of very wealthy men was actually the mastermind behind this cascade of tragic events. They had been carefully cultivating men, institutions and policies for more than 100 years to get to this point. The tragedy that was now inundating our country was the culmination of decades of their careful planning and work. Their intent was to use all of this suffering to bring the United States of America, and all its wealth, under their immediate control. Even our dictator-president had been carefully chosen and groomed for his place in this scenario. They also had never trusted our military to fully do their dirty work. They knew another force might be needed to do this. For this reason, they had encouraged UN troops to be stationed in the United States. It was ostensibly done in the name of coordinating our forces with the UN forces. They said they would train our combined militaries for peacekeeping roles around the world. However, this was just a cover to get the UN troops into the United States, so that they would already be here when they were needed. These troops came with all kinds of equipment. We paid for most of it. Imagine that. As a nation, we had been so completely deceived by the falsely compassionate lie of how wonderful the socialist dream was, that we had willingly given our own money to promote those programs that were then being used against us. We had indeed provided the money to purchase the rope with which we were to be hanged. This sounded a lot like something Marx had said a long time ago. This secret cadre of wealthy men now let our president know that he was to use these UN troops to enforce their programs.

Since our own military had proven less than dedicated in this endeavor up until now, the President did as he was told. He asked for help from these UN troops that were already on our soil. These troops gladly complied. They had no allegiance to the Constitution and had no compunction about shooting American citizens. By late June and early July, these troops were mobilized all over the country. The President ordered some special units into the Mountain West. They moved into the Wasatch Front. If we had thought our lot hard before, they now instituted a ruthless and deliberate plan of attack against the Church and its members. Raids were held everywhere in the large cities. By this time most of the faithful saints were already gone into the safe areas of refuge, but there were some who were slow in going, and now found themselves in grave danger. Many of these people died at the hands of the UN troops. The slaughter was horrible; blood ran in the streets.

As this new phase was starting, the Church moved all of its records out of the Salt Lake City area and took them south and east to a prepared place for safe keeping. For the first time in several generations, the center of the Church was not in Salt Lake City, but elsewhere. The State of Utah now found itself with two groupings of citizens. One was centered on the Wasatch Front under the control of FEMA, with the military, which was now augmented by UN troops. The Edmunds Initiative was their guide and law. The other group had its allegiance to the government of Christ that now controlled the expanding safe areas. Their influence extended from parts of Canada to Northern Mexico, and they were located almost exclusively in the Mountain West. These people felt that the evil coming out of Washington, D.C. was repugnant. They were determined to reestablish the Constitution in its original form. They wanted the United States of America to be among those nations that survived to go into the millennial reign of Christ. They knew it would have to bring itself into compliance with the laws of the government of Christ in order to do that. These people represented a solid core of righteous men and women. They now called a new constitutional convention from among those people who were still free.

This solid core of righteous men and women came together from around the West, a West now isolated by chaos and war from the rest of the country. This group was reminiscent of the inspired Founding Fathers who wrote the Constitution. They had all witnessed first hand the destructive and oppressive consequences of the big government policies that had come from Washington DC. They saw the horrible price of socialist laws and philosophy as they destroyed the individual and the traditional family. These were honest men and women who were determined that would never happen again. They also saw how the divine guiding hand of Christ had saved us from the crushing hand of evil government.

Therefore, when they met in the new Constitutional Convention, they immediately set about the task of restoring the Constitution in its original form. They did not begin by writing new laws. Rather, they systematically went through and repealed law after law. The government bureaucracy was dissolved to a tiny skeleton of its former bloated self. Most of the Amendments to the Constitution were repealed except the Bill of Rights and the prohibition on slavery. One amendment was added guaranteeing that Christ, and all having to do with him, would now be an everyday part of life in America, from business to education to government. No more was restriction allowed in any form on the free and open discussion of God in public. No more would the government do anything for people which they could do for themselves or handle locally. Indeed, the federal government handled only defense and a few interstate issues on a very limited basis. No more excursions into other nation's affairs. No more United Nations. No more Federal Reserve or income tax. All financing for the federal government would come from import/export duties when stability returned. The National Park System was repealed and all federal lands were given to the states, thus allowing a tax base sufficient to support the now very limited state government needs. The state governments went through and followed this same pattern of massive downsizing. Truly, our freedoms were restored and people were now asking, as Isaiah did, "Where is the scribe? Where is the receiver? Where is he that counted the towers?" Isaiah 33:18. The best part of all was that Christ was meeting personally with the Prophet and apostles, and with some of the Saints. He was guiding us as a people and preparing us to go back to Missouri and build the New Jerusalem.

It was important to note that these events involving the Savior were not His Second Coming. He would yet come in glory in the clouds of heaven and all would see Him together. No, these visits by Christ were not that event. These were only a few of the many "smaller" visits that were needed to prepare the way for His Second Coming. Many thought that after Christ's resurrection, He would not appear again until his Second Coming, but this was false. Did not Christ appear numerous times to His apostles after his resurrection? Did He not appear to Paul and Stephen after His ascension? Did He not appear to thousands upon thousands of the people here in the Americas after He left Palestine? Did He not appear many times to the Prophet Joseph Smith in the process of restoring His Priesthood and Church to the earth in this last dispensation? And has He not appeared to many of the prophets and apostles since the time of Joseph Smith as He has guided the Church in our day?

Even so, He was appearing then to the Prophet and apostles, and even some of the Saints, as He directed the establishment of His earthly political kingdom, and as He guided the work for the establishment for these cities of refuge. All these visits were by way of preparation for His coming in glory later.

The results of the new Constitutional Convention were electrifying. Copies of the now restored Constitution were sent all over the country and the world. Up and down the Mountain West, citizens of the different states came together for their own state constitutional conventions. They followed the pattern set by the new Constitutional Convention. They repealed all parts that violated the government of Christ and His laws. They incorporated guarantees of religious free speech and religious involvement in daily life. All state bureaucracies were slashed into tiny shells of their former selves, and all liberties were restored to the people. Severe restrictions were placed on the powers of the state governments. The sigh of relief was almost audible!

As word spread to the rest of the country of what was happening in the West, there was consternation in Washington, D.C. It was not supposed to go like this. The Washington power structure and their secret masters were aware that this breath of freedom was quite capable of ruining everything they had accomplished so far. They knew that if this movement for freedom got a toehold, it would eventually grow and replace them. After all, freedom has a way of being infectious and successful; so they plotted its demise.

At the same time, lovers of freedom from outside the West began to look to the mountains for their light and inspiration. What they saw gave them hope. They figured if it could happen in the West, it could happen in their area, too. However, they turned out to be only a minority of the people in those areas. So a deliberate attempt to get to the West began for many of those lovers of freedom. Indeed, as the situation across the country worsened, a population switch began to occur; lovers of freedom going West, and those trusting the Washington government going east. This was to speed up as time went on.

Now in Utah a new state government had been instituted and an election was held for all state officers. This occurred within the safe areas of the state that were controlled by the government of Christ. Immediately, the new officers were sworn in, with a new governor, new legislature, and new judges. They went through and began enforcing all provisions of the new state Constitution. They passed laws transferring all state property of Utah into their hands and informed the people in Salt Lake City that they were released, that their laws were void, and commanded them to vacate all state property immediately. All who ignored their commands would be treated as trespassers or worse. This same pattern occurred in all the western states. New constitutions were passed and new state officials were elected. All of the old governments that were now controlled by the FEMA people were revoked and ordered to leave!

Representatives from each of these western states then met and ratified the new, restored, national Constitution. They were delighted that it was back in its original form. Elections were held and a new congress was elected and a new electoral college was chosen. The electoral college set about finding a president for the once again United States of America. An honorable and honest man was chosen to be president. He was very spiritual and worked hand in hand with the kingdom of God. He brought wisdom and strength to our cause.

The Lord had another surprise in store. He revealed this in July. He now opened the hidden mineral wealth of the western mountains. Huge reserves of gold and silver were revealed to righteous men for the purpose of helping the Saints to establish a new economic system. This new system was to provide relief for the Saints individually, and it was to allow the Church and the Kingdom of God to function independently of the world. When the wealthy men of the secret group saw that a new economic system was forming that was outside of the one they controlled, they were panicked and made many threats, which were ignored. The new system was based on gold as a medium of exchange. It also was not debt based, but rather was equity based through the law of consecration. This prevented large amounts of production from being eaten up by interest payments. This one change alone made the system very effective and powerful.

The Dictator President, back in Washington, D.C. could not have been more amazed. He threatened us and said he would crush this government in exile that was now growing in the West

As for the Church, it was stronger than ever, though much smaller. Less than a third of those who previously called themselves members had finally chosen to follow Christ and his prophets, but those who did were dedicated and were sacrificing all for their Savior and their fellow men. The Church had temporarily pulled out of Salt Lake City proper, but later it would return after the full cleansing by the Lord was done in that area. For now, events were rapidly coming to a head.

House Upon The Sand

CHAPTER 7

THE NATION

By this point, it was July; nine months had elapsed since the October collapse. Outside of the West, the chaos had been growing unabated since February. At that point, the President's men had some control of the coastal areas, but were having less success in the Midwest and South. In the coastal states, with their large metropolitan areas, the military and FEMA intervened with a vengeance. In LA, Portland, Boston, New York, Miami and other cities, military rule was immediately established. Curfews were instituted and all rioters were shot on sight. All elected officials and bureaucrats were required to accept the Edmunds Initiative. This was for the state, county and city levels. They had to swear loyalty to the President. Then they were given their national identity cards.

Initially there were quite a few who objected. However, anyone who objected to this order was arrested and whisked away. At first, no one was quite sure of what happened to these people, but it was rumored that they were sent to be "re-educated." Over time, there was mounting evidence that everyone who stood in the way of the Initiative in these areas ended up in one of the camps. Those who were sent to these re-education camps never came back. Because of this, all outward opposition to the Initiative fell silent. Fear and intimidation had its desired effect and the coastal states fell in line, however reluctantly.

Other more pliant people quickly surfaced who were more than willing to parrot the President's line. Smiling photo moments of FEMA, the military and the new local leaders were broadcast over all the local news stations along both coasts, showing how well the Initiative was going. Military protection of all food shipping was instituted, so convoys of food began moving again into the large cities. Farmers were ordered back on their farms to get food production up and running. They were guaranteed a good price for their food in an attempt to motivate production. This was necessary since the commodity markets were still down, and since the lack of money was keeping demand so low that prices still were down. The problem was that tax revenues were now so low that the Federal Reserve was actually authorizing the printing of dollars which it then loaned directly to the government at interest in an attempt to prime the economy. Some of that money was diverted to the farmers. That meant the rest of the money was going out for a few government services. The main checks being paid were to the military and the federal bureaucracy. This was done to keep them loyal to the President. Some social security checks still went out but were no longer sufficient to meet the people's needs. These social security checks had been reduced along with the wage/price collapse.

Business in general was very slow. Sometimes it was actually nonexistent. In some areas the violence of the past two months had brought everything to a halt. Notwithstanding the orders from FEMA to go back to work, companies were still having trouble opening their doors. Many of them had suffered huge losses in the riots, and others just had no buyers anymore for what they produced. This left the administrators of the Initiative in the awkward position of trying to push a consumer-based economy which had no buyers. It was like trying to push a string; it just did not work.

Even the import/export business was dead. The collapse of the American economic engine months before had the effect of torpedoing all those recovering economies around the world. They could not sell to us because we were not buying, and we could not sell to them because they had lost their jobs, and therefore had no buying power either. The stagnation of the world economy was now turning into contraction. This was occurring in the United States as well. The coastal states with their big cities were at least "quiet," although it was an uneasy and artificial quiet.

FEMA established its control centers everywhere and required all citizens to register and receive the same national identity card that their leaders had accepted. For the "safety" of the country, all were required to take the same loyalty oath. Once again there was some opposition, but all who did oppose were identified. After awhile, people noticed that certain of their neighbors were being taken away. These were the same people who opposed what the President was doing. Often, in the middle of the night, military or paramilitary groups would show up and take people away. Usually, they took whole families: fathers, mothers and children. Horror stories began trickling back about what happened to these folks. It was rumored that they, too, were sent to the re-education camps. Stories of torture, rape and death began surfacing. As evidence mounted that these stories were true, people in the coastal areas turned their heads the other way. No one was willing to risk getting sent to these places. The general line was "there is no real evidence" that those atrocities were happening. Then, in the next sentence, they would say, "Besides, they brought it on themselves." The cowardice and hypocrisy were sickening.

The few that still had the courage of their convictions went into hiding. These people heard of the valiant resistance going on out in the Mountain West, and many began moving that direction. They moved mostly at night and on foot. Travel restrictions were in place, and so this proved very hazardous. Only a few were able to get out safely. All who were caught were sent to the "camps."

By June, the UN troops were mobilized in these areas in a small way. Generally, their help was not much required in these coastal areas because the local populations were primarily under control. At this time FEMA announced the new and improved national identity method; the injectable identity chip. It had taken some time to get enough of these to do the job, but that was now accomplished. A systematic placement of the chip under the skin of the hand began in all the areas controlled by the dictator president. All FEMA centers notified people that they were to return with their national identity cards and receive the chip instead. Everyone was informed that without the identity chip, they could not work, they could not obtain food, and business could not operate. It all sounded much like the mark of the beast prophesied in the Book of Revelations, only now it was not some distant threat. It was very real and immediate.

In the cities of the Midwest and South, the people did not receive the Initiative well at all. They spoke openly of rejecting the President's plan. Many of the elected officials who had escaped from Washington, D.C. in January were leading a resistance to the President in their respective areas. Military units loyal to the Constitution had broken away from the national military command structure. These units were isolated and there was no central command organization coordinating this resistance, either militarily or politically. It was every state for itself, and it became worse. Within each state, the counties and cities were not cooperating well. The financial chaos and civil turmoil had put food distribution and business trade on a tenuous footing. Each local area felt like it had to take care of itself, and so February and March of that year were best described as chaotic and dangerous. There were still areas of rioting; roving mobs were still heard of also, especially around the large cities. States as diverse as Illinois and Louisiana, or Iowa and Alabama were experiencing similar problems. Large-scale starvation was beginning as distribution became spotty. Each state attempted to protect what food production it had while hoping to get added food shipments from other areas. The National Guard units in these areas were loyal to their states and were still being used to maintain order, but now they were being augmented by the breakaway national military units as well.

All this was causing concern that the union of the country was breaking up. States, counties and cities in these areas of the Midwest and South were somewhat civil with one another, but the old rules of interaction were failing. Free and open movement of food and products was greatly impeded by the civil unrest, by fear and by suspicion. In addition, these states looked with contempt on the east and west coast states that had rolled over so easily for the dictatorship. The only thing that could be said for these coastal areas was that they were at least somewhat unified, even if it was under martial law.

However, the President was not without influence in the central part of the country. Even though some national military units had broken away, most had stayed loyal to him. Because of the purges, General Stevenson had gained control of most of the national military. Almost all of the military bases were under the President's control. In addition, all the FEMA people had been purged and were determined to see the President's plan work. These FEMA leaders had succeeded in tying up the limited federal funds and were trying to bribe and threaten the local governments with this money.

Last but not least, even though there was great resistance and open rebellion in this central part of the country, there were still plenty of people there who were willing to go along with the President's plan. These people did this for their own selfish gain. There are almost always people like this hidden in a large population. They await an opportunity to gratify their desire for power, greed and lust. This was just such an opportunity. So you see, the President easily found allies who came crawling out of the woodwork, each one willing to engage in some intrigue that was mutually beneficial for the President and them. These people began quietly working with FEMA and the military.

Lack of unity among these Midwestern and southern states left them vulnerable to a coordinated attack by the forces of the Edmunds Initiative. Previous purges had left a command structure of ruthless men and women within the President's program. They were cunning and clever, in the worldly sense. They knew they were vastly outnumbered in this central and southern part of the country; but they also knew how to use treachery, division, threats and lies, to get their way. A four-part plan was put into place. It went something like this. First, they would defeat the main military forces of the resistance. Second, they would cut off the large cities and isolate them. Third, they would replace these rebel leaders with local people acceptable to the President. And fourth, they would occupy the large cities. Following these actions, there would just be a mop-up job for the rest of the areas in each state.

The President's FEMA leaders identified prominent people in each state who had expressed a desire to be part of the Initiative. Secret meetings were held with each of these people in late March and early April. They were carefully trained in how to impose and administer the Edmunds Initiative. They gave their loyalty oath, and it was determined that they were capable of the kind of ruthless enforcement needed to carry out the plan. These people were each told to be available by May for a change of leadership that would place them in power.

Next, the national military leaders used their intelligence capabilities to locate all the rebel forces. These rebel military units had taken control of a few bases, and the remainder were centered near the big cities; like Chicago, St. Louis, New Orleans, Cincinnati, and Minneapolis/St. Paul, to mention just a few. Then, in mid-April, a coordinated series of air strikes began against all major rebel units. The bases were hit hardest, even though the units around the cities were hit as well. The first waves of strikes destroyed so much military hardware that the rebels found themselves in a position of not being able to effectively strike back. They now had to take a mostly defensive position. The air strikes continued, and by the end of April, marine and army units moved aggressively forward, and seized all the bases. This greatly demoralized the remaining rebel units all over the Midwest and South.

They were counting on those bases for their supplies, and now the supplies were gone. The loss of life as American fought American was tragic. Indeed, the cost in life was very high. About this same time, other marine and army units attacked those rebel forces around the larger cities. Tanks, helicopters, planes, bombs and numberless concourses of men seemed to descend on each chosen area. The fighting was fierce as the national military pursued the rebels through the streets of the cities they were trying to protect. Explosions and gunfire, the dead and the dying, seemed to fill these cities. People who had once prided themselves on their manicured lawns and beautiful landscaping, now found armed soldiers running through their yards, killing anyone who resisted their advance. Mostly, they just were after the rebel military, but they soon found that many locals still had guns, and often these citizens were willing to use them. The national military units made a point of executing these people, and would blow up their homes as a warning to anyone else who felt the need to fire on them. As the days of fighting wore on around these cities, the smoke of numerous fires was visible. It soon became apparent to the governors and mayors of these areas that open resistance was not going to work. To make matters worse, the rioting and mobs which had died down for a while, now broke out again. The fighting had disrupted what minimal services had been operating, and all food distribution had stopped again. This caused more starvation and desperation, which seemed to play into the national military leaders' hands. They actually had hoped for this result and played on it now. Other cities, not yet attacked, knew their turn was coming and knew that the end results would be the same. Reasonable people in all these areas spoke out in favor of some kind of agreement to halt the fighting.

In the middle of May, FEMA and the national military leaders called for negotiations. "Let's stop this destruction and bloodshed," they said. "We are brothers and sisters. Surely we can work something out." The desire for compromise was born of desperation, and the governors, mayors and other local leaders in each state agreed to meet with the President's men. Since all of these states were functioning separately, the meetings were set up separately. This actually was in the best interest of the plan laid out by the leaders of the Edmunds Initiative. Divide and conquer is still true. Secretly, all the national leaders had arranged among themselves to use the same date for their meetings. It was to be May 15. Each state meeting was then set up on that same date. This was done so that no one state could warn the others of what was happening.

The FEMA and national military people selected sites that seemed neutral, but which were actually very accessible to their troops. Special forces units were hidden within these locations and back up units were close by waiting to pounce. Unfortunately, the rebel military and the local and state leaders did not know of this treachery, having never dealt with something like this before. Representatives of FEMA, the national military, the rebel military, the state governments, the county and city governments, and many prominent local citizens were all invited to these meetings for the so-called "negotiations." The prominent local citizens were actually the people FEMA had trained to lead the governments of these states, counties and cities when the rebel leaders were out of the way.

The day of the meetings had arrived. Twenty different states were involved and so there were twenty different meeting locations. Within each state across the Midwest and the South, people began to gather at the buildings where the peace was to be negotiated. Little did the local leaders know that the only peace there would be was the President's peace. As the meetings began, all seemed well. Each side was given time to express their grievances and make suggestions on what might be done to make things better. As the day wore on, the talks appeared to be going well to the participants in each state.

Then the trap was sprung. A luncheon was set and all adjourned from their meetings. All the FEMA, national military and prominent replacement people had been coached before the meeting, that on a set signal they were to separate themselves from the rest of the people at the meeting. This they did on cue, at which time the special forces seized the banquet halls and surrounded all the state, local and rebel military leaders. At the same time, the regular military units that were nearby swooped down and took control of each area where the meetings were being held. Trucks were brought in, in preparation for transporting the rebels and the disloyal local leaders away.

Inside the building, the FEMA people invoked the powers given them by the Edmunds Initiative. They accused all the state, local and rebel military leaders of being traitors and they placed them under military arrest. A quick trial was held at each spot. It resembled a kangaroo court more than any legal action we were accustomed to. Accusations had already been drawn up, witnesses of FEMA's choosing were waiting nearby and judgment was handed down on each group. No individual trials were held. They were accused, tried and judged as a group. The accusations were treason. The verdict was guilty, and the punishment was death. All this occupied only about two hours of time.

By late afternoon, the "convicted traitors" were tied and led away to the waiting trucks. They were loaded in like cattle and hauled away to the camps. At this time, crews of military moved into the cities and arrested the families of these men and women and took them away. They also had a list of prominent and important citizens who had supported the rebels and opposed the President. Most of the people on this list were also arrested, along with their families. All of them were trucked away to the camps. None of these people were ever seen again. Reports did trickle back that they had been tortured and killed. This information was actually leaked by FEMA itself to instill fear in the population.

Back at the meeting places, the people who had been groomed to fill all the leadership spots in these states were sworn in as the new governors, mayors, councilmen and local leaders. Backed by the national military, they moved into the government buildings of each of these states and took over.

By the morning of May 16, word of what had happened was all over the Midwest and South. Only a few small groups had the presence of mind to move quickly to get out of harm's way. Those leaders who had been missed the day before went into hiding. Others who disagreed with the President's Initiative began moving west while they still could. They had heard that a well-organized group out there was defending the Constitution with some success. They desired to join them. Everywhere else, confusion reigned and most people did not know what to do. This was the result that FEMA had counted on.

The replacement government people were put into place. Actually, they were little more than puppets. Nevertheless, this gave an air of legitimacy to the takeover of each of these states by the Dictator President's people. The main TV and radio stations were seized; prepared announcements began airing, that said, in essence, that the negotiations were a success. They said that peace was restored and that all traitors in the leadership had been dealt with. They announced the names of the new "loyal" government officials who would now help heal the wounds of each state.

People were not stupid. They knew what had happened. Generally, they just did not know what to do. As for May 15, it is now a day that will live in infamy. It carries with it all the weight and sorrow of both treachery and massacre. Everywhere, lovers of freedom mourned for what had occurred. Word of this deceit soon reached the West, but out here we were struggling with our own crisis of oppression, persecution, lies, deaths and general suffering. However, at the same time, we were starting the cities of refuge, and Christ had established His kingdom. We were just not yet in a position to offer help. That would come later. A glimmer of hope was starting to show in the West. It just needed time to grow into the brilliant light of truth and freedom it was destined to become.

Around the Midwest and South, the back of the organized resistance to the Edmunds Initiative had been broken. That did not mean it was going to be easy to force the Dictator President's will on those twenty states. The populations in these states were not nearly as easy to intimidate as the "liberal minded" people of the coastal states had been. Most of these states were much more conservative in their general thinking. They were more independent by nature, and had a strong love for Constitutional principles and for freedom. Individual resistance popped up everywhere. An underground resistance began immediately. It was made up of those previous government officials who had gone into hiding, when FEMA replaced all of the elected officials with its people. The underground was also made up of the rebel military men and women who had gone into hiding when their military units collapsed with the death of all their commanders on May 15. They took with them all the weapons, ammunition, bombs and various hardware they could. They also destroyed all the tanks, trucks and planes they had to leave behind. They did not want these things to be used against them later.

By the end of May, FEMA had its centers up and running full bore. They had seized all of the TV, radio and press businesses in each state. All press releases of any kind were censored and a blitz of pro-Initiative and pro-President ads were being broadcast. The military had secured all the cities, major towns and transportation hubs. Each citizen was now ordered to present himself at these FEMA centers, and receive a national identity chip. As they had done elsewhere, they required all to take a loyalty oath. They began injecting the ID chips right away, since they now had enough to do the job. It was only a few weeks after this that they instituted the same program on the coasts and in the west. Again, anyone who wanted food or a job, or who wanted to run a business had to have a chip. Curfews were instituted, and anyone violating curfew was arrested. Anyone rioting was shot on sight. A general confiscation of guns was started by the military and paramilitary units. This was at the beginning of June. This led to many gun fights as people resisted.

Many in the military who had supported their leaders in taking over these twenty states from the rebels, now found it hard to fire on nonmilitary people. These were average citizens claiming their Constitutional rights and these military men had some sympathy for them. They did not feel good about what they saw as an inappropriate action by their military leaders. It was one thing to attack rebels who threatened the union, but it was an entirely different thing to attack regular, law-abiding citizens. For this reason, enforcement of some of the Initiative's regulations did not go well.

Because of the chaos of the last few months, only a few farmers had planted crops. The extremely low commodity prices, the widespread bank foreclosures on farms, the roving mobs and the uncertainty of the future had led many farmers not to plant. This led to a major reduction in the harvest for that fall. As the

President's leaders gained control in the breadbasket of America, they found a situation with fields only partly planted, and many farms abandoned or damaged by mobs. They ordered all farmers to plant, and as they had done on the coasts, promised them a good price for their crops. They began to funnel some money to them in an attempt to get food production going again. In order for any leader to remain in power, he must be able to feed his population, or he will not last long. This old truth was not lost on our Dictator President and his minions. The only people you starve to death are your enemies. After all, you plan to kill them anyway, so it does not matter if they die. Since the rioting and mobs were largely under control now, many farmers responded and went back to their farms. Still, it was obvious that the harvest would fall far short of previous years.

There was another problem that was more widespread. The downward financial spiral that began in October was still moving unabated. By that June, the financial infrastructure of the country was a shambles. All that credit that had been created had found its most excessive expression in the use of derivatives. Not too long ago, people of importance in our financial leadership were singing the praises of wealth creation through derivatives and hedge funds. Even the leaders at the Federal Reserve were saying what a good thing this was. They placed an estimated value of eighty trillion dollars on these derivatives, and then gave them their blessing. When the collapse began in October, all that "wealth," all that "credit," started to come down. It had been created by incredible amounts of leveraging (a type of borrowing) which suddenly came due. Financial numbers as high as eighty trillion dollars are impossible to fully collateralize, and so any situation that would turn those funds into a significant loss would cause them to fail. When failures of that magnitude occur, they are not isolated events, and they affect everything around them. The previous fall was a classic example of this.

As the collapse gained speed in that fateful October, and again in the November that followed, fund after fund went under. Many trillions of dollars in credit and wealth evaporated overnight, along with everything that was connected to them.

Banks, investment houses, mutual funds, insurance companies, and government agencies had all been drinking at the trough of these hedge funds with their derivatives. These losses were more than these institutions could handle. As the derivatives and hedge funds sank, they dragged everything around them under, like the Titanic. People lost their savings, their retirements, their homes, their businesses, and their futures. In those last manic months of greed before October, many had leveraged everything they had to get in on the "chance" for wealth. They did not want to miss that boat. They just did not realize it was the Titanic.

The dollar started down and had been devalued by more than 85% by June. All foreign goods were very expensive by now as a result. Most people did not have any money to buy anything at all. Trade was almost at a standstill. As that October slid into January and then June, most banks failed and closed their doors permanently. The same was true of the insurance companies that had been hit with a double whammy by the hedge fund failures and the big earthquakes in November. They too were mostly closed by now. The investment houses were either closed or tiny shadows of their former selves. For the most part, the mutual funds were bankrupt and closed also. As for the government agencies, they too, were hit hard. Their bonds were essentially worthless by June. As a result of all this, no lending in any form to anyone or any organization was occurring anywhere. Those banks that were still open were afraid to lend for fear they would not be repaid.

Finally, to add insult to injury, gold had been steadily climbing and was at almost $1000 per ounce. All that talk that gold was no longer perceived as money and that a fiat currency was the wave of the future had been proven wrong. No one wanted paper money if something more substantial, like gold, was available. That was what they wanted. It was readily apparent to all that the dollar would soon be worthless unless something was done soon. This was worsened by the fact that the Federal Reserve had arranged for the printing of dollars to make up for the shortfall in tax revenues. The President and his financial advisors were now considering going back to a gold standard to save the dollar.

The more immediate and pressing problem was that business in general was not doing well. Manufacturing was almost at a standstill and smaller businesses were only slightly better. In a debt-based system, it is critical to get consumer credit flowing again, but the government did not know how to do that. With all their learning, they did not know what to do. So the Dictator President and his leaders tried to talk people into thinking things were getting better. They hoped this would start people buying again. It all proved to be a waste of time.

The stubborn resistance of people in the Midwest and South was a problem more easily solved. In June, the UN troops were called out to help in those twenty states. They took over where the United States military had proven reluctant. They started with gun seizures. They were not squeamish about shooting people who resisted. Round ups began which brought everyone in to be registered and to receive their national identity chip. At gunpoint, loyalty oaths were taken, chips received, and people given work assignments. This was so that they could do their "patriotic" duty to serve their country in its time of need. Some people refused the loyalty oath and were summarily executed on the spot. This was intended to instill fear in all who watched.

Even with the oppressive hand of a dictatorial government now gaining ground everywhere, except in the Mountain West, there was much resistance. Guerrilla strikes and bombings were occurring constantly. Some of the President's previously loyal troops were secretly helping the underground resistance. It was not uncommon by July to hear of government buildings being blown up, or to see monuments defaced, or to hear of small military groups being ambushed. Soon all UN troops and US troops had to travel in large groups for protection. The underground actually began assassinating the leaders of the Initiative.

The situation with the Indians was a different story. Generally, their populations were concentrated around a widely scattered system of reservations. When they were conquered more than

100 years ago, treaties were signed that made certain promises to them. They expected these treaties to be kept. They also had their own governments. In the last few decades, the governing councils for the Indian groups had learned how to use the court system of the United States of America to enforce their treaty rights. More and more of the Indians were becoming highly educated and sophisticated in their dealings with the US Government. They also were operating their own businesses and industries. Now with this crisis, the promises made long ago to them were once again being broken. They were low on the government's priority list, and as the funds dried up, the promised payments to the tribes stopped. Unlike most of the people in the country, who had no large family structure or resources to fall back on, the Indians viewed themselves as nations or peoples with rights that were separate from the federal government. They had inherited these rights from their ancestors. This included the right to their lands, to their families and to run their own government. They also had their own traditions, or religious beliefs, that told them that the day would come when the white government would be destroyed. At that day, they expected to rise up and become a great people again. To them, this collapse was not unexpected.

Now the tribes found themselves on their own. They did not accept the Edmunds Initiative; instead they called a council of all the Indian tribes in the United States and Canada. This council was to act as a coordinating body for intertribal decisions and actions. Each tribe acted individually to meet its own needs. Some tribal councils initiated their own food purchases when possible. Other tribes had the capacity to grow their own food, which they immediately set about doing. Others organized hunting groups to obtain meat the old fashioned way. Industries were initiated to meet clothing and shelter needs.

Regarding the Indians, something else occurred. The government dole, that had bred indigence for some Indian groups, was now gone. If these Indian groups were to survive, they had to do for themselves. Inherent ingenuity and intelligence of the Indians began to blossom in this new environment. The

Indian tribes found themselves divided somewhat into two groups. One group emphasized peaceful development, and wanted to try to get along with the whites around them. To some extent, they felt sorry for the whites as they saw their suffering. The other group, usually populated by the younger Indians, wanted to organize themselves militarily, take back their ancestral lands, and reassert their authority. This group armed itself and began to make the sounds of war. Their saber rattling actually concerned the groups of peaceful Indians. It also concerned some of the whites outside the reservations who saw what was happening. They realized this had the potential to become a big problem. For some reason that is not entirely clear to me, our Dictator President ignored the Indians. I suppose he thought them not worthy of his attention, or perhaps he thought they would support him. In either case, he would have been very wrong. They were organized, intelligent, talented and determined.

Among all those who rejected the Edmunds Initiative, the only other group of people who were as organized and cohesive as the Indians were the Mormons. The Church leaders also were doing things for the good of our people, such as the aggressive development of food production, the promotion of home and general industries to meet the needs of the people, and the promotion of a peaceful and free government based on Constitutional principles. Also, Christ's political government had been established on earth, and it was prospering and growing.

In July, formal ties were opened between the government of Christ in the Mountain West and the Indian nations that were not already involved in building the cities of refuge. They too were asked to accept His rule. Christ told them that it was He who visited their ancestors. He was the white god; He was the prophet spoken of in so many of their legends. It was He who healed the wounds of their forefathers. It was He who moved the mountains, calmed the winds, walked on the waters and tamed the wild beasts almost 2000 years before. He said that He had promised their ancestors that He would return, and now He was back.

This news was received with disbelief by most of the Indian groups. They did not know what to think. Angry voices complained that the call to them was coming from the white man's home in the Mormon Nation, as they called it. They could not see how that could be true. Other, calmer voices, said that their visions had already shown them that they would stand side by side with the Mormons; that Mormons and Indians would work together to serve the white god. The disagreement between these two groups was not solved at that time. Many of these Indians had their own ideas about how the legends and prophesies were to be fulfilled. When it did not happen exactly as they had envisioned it would, they were upset. We must be careful that we do not reject God's plan just because it does not always happen as we expect. His ways are not our ways. Many of the Indian leaders already understood this principle. Therefore, many of the tribes did decide to send delegations to the cities of refuge to meet with Christ, to see if, indeed, He was the prophesied one.

On the international scene, things were mayhem. When the President had called all our troops home some eight or nine months ago, the international balance of power, that other nations were depending upon the US to maintain, fell apart. The numerous base closings were a financial disaster for many countries, but that was small compared to the suppressed hatred, ambitions and greed that were turned loose by our military withdrawal. Many nations felt betrayed by us. We had promised to defend them. For that reason, they had not attempted in any real way to build their own militaries. Suddenly they were left as sitting ducks for age-old enemies around them. Ancient and modern hatreds now resurfaced. These had been kept in check by our previous military presence, but now that was gone.

In vain, the United States of America promised to keep its treaty obligations. It said it would be faithful to NATO, SEATO, the UN and its nuclear promises. These were empty words. The military presence necessary for such treaties was gone, or was so severely diminished that the promises could not be kept.

At first, the nations of the world watched in disbelief as America self-destructed before their eyes. We had been so united and so powerful for so long that it was inconceivable that the United States could lose its unity. Now, they saw a surreal landscape of economic chaos, famine, suffering, and finally civil war. It did not seem possible for these things to happen in the country that was the envy of the world only a few years before.

As the external restraints imposed on these nations by the previous international system evaporated, these countries and groups eyed one another warily. Initially, the status quo was honored by default. The alternative of chaos and war was not very desirable to most; and the principle of inertia kept things going the way they were, at least for a while. However, in every country there were plenty of people who were ready and willing to challenge that inertia with their own vision of the future. Invariably, their version of the way things should be had them in charge of things at someone else's expense. Of course, they never presented things that way to their people. Instead, they would speak deceptively of helping their people, of righting some past wrong, or of gaining some advantage for their country or group. To accomplish this, their people had only to support and help them, and then they said all would be well. It had an all-too-familiar ring. Such ideas had been spoken hundreds of times in the recent and distant past, and had resulted in tremendous suffering and bloodshed. Often, it was done in the name of God, which was a terrible form of hypocrisy, bordering on blasphemy.

At the time of the collapse in October, there were already numerous "little wars" going on around the world. These had been mostly ignored or avoided, as they served little purpose for the wealthy nations. The real trouble did not begin to surface until about three months later, in January and February. By that time, the nations realized that the old system was probably gone for good. They could see that the United States of America was not going to be interfering again with anyone for a long time, if ever. The opportunistic side of leaders all over the world came out. Artificial boundaries set up after

World War II were brought into question. Areas of influence held by Western Europe and the United States were now being spoken for by old nations with ancient designs. These old nations had long traditions of once being great empires, and now they saw a chance to get some of that power back. This would prove to be an intoxicating and irresistible idea to these countries. We now know it also proved to be short lived and deadly. What began as their hope, ended up being their destruction. The little embers of a xenophobic and greedy nationalism, if fanned, always become as a raging fire that consumes all in its path, including those who fanned the embers into flame in the first place.

We now saw leaders in Russia, China and the Islamic states speak of their past greatness. Each in turn alluded to their superior place on the road of history. They spoke of their need to lead the world and of their need to right injustices done by past treaties and wars. By February, major changes were surfacing throughout the world economically, politically and culturally.

Financially, the economic collapse of the United States of America had dried up the world's last bastion of stability and trade. All the world was tied into our economic system and was depending on us to help them. With that stability now gone, we saw most of the stock markets worldwide drop precipitously. Wealth destruction, and the deflationary consequences of this event hit these countries almost as hard as it hit the US. Unemployment rose rapidly. Trade slowed to a trickle and the currency markets were in chaos. The paper money system of the world was in desperate need of a safe haven. The one thing that seemed to gain attention was gold. Only a few countries had gold reserves sufficient to back their currencies. All that previous talk of selling off the gold reserves of the world now stopped. The few places with significant gold reserves now used them to prop up their currencies. This fact was not lost on the investors of the world as these currencies appreciated rapidly and the dollar plunged. The central banks of some of these countries had been leasing or loaning out some of their gold.

The amounts were in the tons. These lease and loan agreements were now called in, in an attempt to protect their reserves and currencies. They did not want to lose the gold they had loaned as this crisis worsened. The result of this call was that the price of gold rose very rapidly against all currencies worldwide, while back in the United States, gold was approaching $1000 per ounce by late summer.

All this confusion in money values made trade even more difficult. It was getting harder to find profitable ways to transfer ones' profits from country to country. The practical side of this was that many businesses around the world went under. This was a universal problem from Asia to Europe, and from Africa to the Americas. Throngs of the unemployed seemed to swell in the large cities of the planet. This did cause unrest and even some rioting, but nothing like what was going on in America. Most of the other countries had strong extended family ties that helped people get through somehow. They also had more authoritarian traditions, which their governments used to keep things at least somewhat stable. Nevertheless, their financial difficulties rapidly translated into real human suffering, which in turn translated into political instability.

Political changes came on the heels of the financial crisis. There is nothing like large throngs of unemployed, hungry and desperate people to motivate changes in a country's policies and leaders. Those evil men who had disguised their true colors before, now showed themselves. In country after country, they spoke beguilingly of helping their people, of correcting the wrongs that had been brought on by this crisis, and of punishing those responsible for this mess. Existing leaders either fell into this line of thinking, or were replaced by people who did. Voices of reason were shouted down and then silenced. Desperation led to policies based on expediency, not truth. Demagogues were the order of the day in Asia, Europe, Africa and the Americas.

Of particular concern were those demagogues with large armies at their disposal, such as China, Russia and the Islamic states. China began talking of its right to territories around it, like Taiwan, Mongolia, and parts of Southeast Asia. Russia began to reassert its influence over Eastern Europe and the independent republics that had broken off the old USSR. Both of these countries still had huge military structures, including nuclear capabilities. Even though the Cold War had supposedly ended years ago, neither China nor Russia had really dismantled their military machines. Rather, they let them appear quiescent to the world so that all would think their expansionist motives were dead. It was a sham. The United States was called the only superpower during those years, but that was a carefully orchestrated deception. There really had been three military superpowers all along. Now that became apparent. The Islamic states reveled in the trials of America and said God was punishing her. They spoke of their right to reclaim the Holy Land again. They spoke of the need to place fundamentalist Islamic regimes in places throughout the Middle East, Central Asia and Africa. Border disputes became common among many countries and military build ups were the order of the day.

As for the United Nations, it was in confusion. All the financial and political changes washed over its members month after month. As winter rolled into spring and then summer, the tension between the member states of the UN grew. Border skirmishes and violations were common, and the ability of the UN to deal with these events was erased. It found itself divided again roughly as before, with Russia, China and the Islamic nations on one side, and the United States, Canada and Western Europe on the other. By summer, it was obvious that trouble was brewing. New leaders and/or more radical policies were in operation in Russia, China and the Middle East. They no longer made any pretense of friendship with the West. They openly blamed Europe and America for the world's problems and were actively building their militaries. These military build-ups gave their countries a temporary boost economically, as the unemployed were put to work building weapons, filling the ranks of the military and doing public works projects to prepare their countries for war.

Pressure was brought to bear on Western Europe and the United States by Russia and China. They said they would use war to obtain their rights unless they were accommodated. By late summer, the West was in no condition to fight a war with either of these countries, and so began a policy of appeasement. This was done even though history showed that appeasement does not work. Demands were made to expand the areas of influence of the Eastern Block countries. This was granted. Demands were made for the United States to withdraw their missiles and other weapons from Europe. This, too, was done. The amazing thing was that the populations of the Western European countries generally agreed with this. Only a few objected. Most said it would be a gesture of good will at a difficult time. They said it would bring peace; they could not have been more wrong. If a bully is encouraged, in the end, the bully just gets more aggressive. That was the case here. Perhaps the greatest tragedy was that troops from many of these hostile countries previously had been invited into the United States of America, and were now being used to help our Dictator President impose his will. The use of UN troops was heartily supported by Russia and China. This later gave them an inroad to our country when World War III broke out. For now, these foreign troops, along with some of our own troops, were being used against good and patriotic Americans everywhere.

Culturally, on the international scene, minority groups found themselves the targets of the demagogues. In Europe it was the African-Arab, Turks and Gypsies who suffered. In China it was the Japanese, Vietnamese, Tibetans and Southeast Asians who suffered. In Russia it was the Jews, Americans and Western Europeans who suffered. In the Islamic world, it was the Hindus, Jews and Americans who suffered. In America it was the Christians and political conservatives who suffered. This of course, is only a sampling of the groups actually targeted, but it gives an idea of what was happening.

As for the secret international group of wealthy men, they were getting concerned as this process rolled forward. It was not going as they had planned and was proving unusually difficult to control. They found that many of the people they had meticulously cultivated and prepared for this time, were now turning on them. They found themselves increasingly targets of the machine they helped create. This is a problem common to most secret groups. Once such a group gets going, invariably, some of the people in the group think they deserve to lead more than their leaders do. Quiet plots began hatching that led to assassinations, intrigues and power struggles. Internationally, we saw this happening, although most of the general population did not understand what was occurring. This weakness for internal dissension within secret groups usually contributes to their failure. That was the case here as well. A few secret leaders of this group began to find themselves being arrested and their property confiscated. Others were more wary and figured they were clever enough to keep it all under their control. This was a fatal miscalculation. However, they did not realize their error until it was too late.

We began to see minority groups migrate across national boundaries, hoping to get to areas of safety. This massive migration was in full swing by early fall. Even in the United States it was occurring, except that it was not based on racial lines. It was based on religious and political lines. One migration that was remarkable because of its sheer size, was the movement of Jews from all over the world to Israel. They took with them their wealth when they could. Israel experienced a huge immigration, and found itself struggling to find housing and food for them all. One thing that helped Israel was the enormous wealth that was also flowing in with this migration. This helped finance some of what was occurring. As a result of this, Israel underwent an economic boom even as other countries were struggling. This only served to create more hard feelings between Israel and its neighbors who were still struggling.

In September of that year, Russia, China and many of the Islamic states of the Middle East and Africa came together in a summit. They formed an alliance. Ostensibly, its purpose was to promote peace between them, promote economic trade, and form a coordinated military structure for the common defense of their shared interests. In reality, this summit was designed to prepare for war against the West, but that was never openly said outside of the summit. The attitude within these countries was that the West, particularly the United States of America, was ripe for the taking. They only needed a plan to carry out this desire.

This plan was put together by the Russian president. He was a polished speaker and an astute politician. He had worked the system and played the public so well that the delegates at this summit made him their leader. He was smooth on the surface, and ruthless underneath. He had the unconditional support of the military and the fawning adoration of the people. You see, he gave them what they thought they needed at a time of crisis. He gave them hope, he gave them jobs and he gave them their pride back. It did not matter that, in the process, they lost what little freedom they had gained. And it did not matter that the road he was going down could only lead to bloodshed and heartache. For the moment, they had "prosperity and national pride." That was enough. This man was very charismatic and his success at home had earned him the attention of other nations, who tried to follow suit. Even the people of Western Europe began to look to this man with admiration. He took the lead at the summit and soon won support for the diabolical plan he was hatching. It all seemed so clear, so right and so justifiable when he said it. The stage was now set for the next step.

CHAPTER 8

THE ATTACK

It was now nine months since the economic collapse. The President's men were consolidating their power over most of the country. Only the West remained untamed to their will. The civil unrest had died down across most of the rest of the country, and there were signs of a tentative recovery, however slight. Food production was up, but still was only half of the previous levels. There was food to eat and starvation was now not so widespread. Some manufacturing was beginning again, and signs of improvement were more visible. The public works projects were giving a little work at least, and the heavy hand of the US and UN military was enforcing the "peace." People generally were complying with the Edmunds Initiative; at least there was no open and organized opposition in the country as a whole, except in the West. Ah yes, that group in the West. We were still a problem. Except for us, the people were accepting the FEMA orders, making the loyalty oaths and receiving the ID chip injections into their hands.

All economic activity was now electronic and some tax flow was occurring. The voluminous records kept by the government were leading their forces to potential rebels wherever they could be found. Once again, government records of all types, such as school records, employment records, political party records, psychological tests, gun registration records, preschool records, early birth and family records were all being evaluated for signs of people who could not be trusted. All who held strong religious beliefs or conservative political views were rounded up. If they were found, they vanished into the work camps and re-education camps, never to be seen again. This process was carried out all over the East Coast, Midwest, South and West Coast. There was a great deal of fear in people; they hoped they would not get a visit from the President's forces. When such a visit did occur, people around them usually looked the other way, for fear of being arrested, too. Anyone who objected to what was happening went into hiding, but that became increasingly difficult as fewer and fewer people were willing to risk their lives to protect them. More and more, they had to go into the wooded areas and wild lands for refuge. These people increasingly looked to the West for safety. They even tried to get to the West when they could.

Across the land, the controlled media sang the now sickening praises of the Dictator President. Propaganda poured out of every radio, TV and newspaper. They were all supporting his plan. The media also attacked all who opposed him. Specifically, it railed against those traitorous "radicals" in the West who were trying to hurt the country. Officials accused all political conservatives and Christians (especially the Mormons) of being the cause of their heartache. It laid at our feet the economic collapse and the food shortages that we had experienced. Our defense of the Constitution was painted as the cause of the violence that wracked the nation; and now we were accused of rebellion and treason for our re-establishment of the Constitution in its original form. We were described in the most heinous terms because we would not submit to the wholesale destruction of our liberty and the creation of a dictatorship. To top everything off, the establishment of the kingdom of Christ to govern the earth was said to be a threat to the peace the UN had achieved. Of course, this was a hollow statement since there was no peace. The world was in turmoil more than ever. For those with eyes to see this outward animosity toward Christ's people was a plain manifestation of the growing divide between good and evil, God and mammon, the kingdom of God and of Babylon. This was prophesied, and so was not unexpected to those who knew the teachings of the prophets.

It was ironic that these patriotic defenders of our liberty and the Constitution would be accused of treason and rebellion. Our accusers in Washington, D.C. were being led by the very people who had sold political influence for foreign money some years before. Those same accusers had declared numerous places in the US as UN sites and were flying the UN flag above the US flag at these American places. And again, these same accusers were the very ones who had invited foreign troops onto our soil, only to use them against our own citizens. And last but not least, those same accusers were the ones who arranged for military technology to be sold to our enemies, making the missile attack we later experienced possible. It should be noted, that technology was given to the very country who donated the most money to our leading politicians years before. This proved to be more than coincidence. It was the height of hypocrisy that those same leaders who had been aiding and abetting our enemies for years, should now accuse those who were staunch defenders of the Constitution of treason.

Treachery, deception and treason had been going on for some time, even within the White House. It was tragic that no one back then had the courage to call these men to task for what they had done. The millions of needless deaths that occurred when the missiles hit our cities later, could have been laid at the feet of our previous and current presidents. These were men who had hoped to secure glowing praise for themselves in the pages of history; now they will be remembered as the Benedict Arnolds of the White House. Even though it might take awhile, the truth always prevails. When it does, people like this are shown for what they really are; such was now the case.

However, at that time, because these truths were not yet widely known and because the missile attack had not yet occurred, the avalanche of propaganda against us was believed to a degree around the country. Persecution began throughout the country against anyone who genuinely believed in Christ and in the Constitution. Neighbors were encouraged to turn in anyone who was suspected of such beliefs. This happened frequently. Whether the accusations were true or not was immaterial. FEMA and the military had the power to arrest those people without a trial. Government officials made a point to catalog all property owned by churches, organizations and individuals who were suspect. This property was then seized. People would wake up on Sunday, dress, and go to church, only to find it locked and guarded. Others would arrive at their places of work to find them closed or under new management. The original owners were either arrested or missing.

By August, the Dictator President was speaking openly of reuniting the country. He invoked the hallowed name of Abraham Lincoln in saying we must be united. He made empty gestures to the new Constitutional government in the West, claiming that if they would accept his government and military rule, all would be forgiven. We knew from the ruthless nature of his conduct in the rest of the country that those statements were lies. First, the May 15 treachery was still fresh on all our minds. Second, we now had the Constitution back in its original form, with all the liberty it offered. Why would we give that up to a socialist dictator? Third, there can be no compromise with evil. To do so leads to destruction.

The President never intended to create a peaceful settlement with the West. He was going through the motions for the sake of appearance so that he could say he had tried. It was a public relations ploy. His real desire was to raise an army to crush the West. His talk of unity, peace and punishment for the West was all just part of his media blitz to get the country ready for military action against the West. He also was preparing to legitimize his coup by holding elections. It was his hope that the new congress would be in place to offer a "ratification" of his war on the West. He intended for this election to occur at its usual time in November. The invasion was then to happen immediately after the election. He had it all planned.

In the Mountain West, a call went out from FEMA and the military for all citizens loyal to the government in Washington, D.C. to leave and move to those states under government control. They said that these loyal citizens would be protected in their travel east, and that temporary places to live would be provided. They were promised that they would not be gone long; as soon as the war of reunification was over, they could return to their homes and lands. The added incentive was provided that they would be given the property of the rebels when they came back to the West after the war, since all who remained were to be annihilated. A media blitz was put out on the state-controlled TV, radio and press. Beginning in late August, and moving into September and October, release after release stated that everyone remaining in the western area controlled by the kingdom of Christ (they called them the "rebel areas") would be killed-man, woman and child. These releases were designed to be as threatening as possible, and repeatedly referred to their military might and technology. Shows of force were made with planes and tanks. A deadline for the completion of the exodus was set for late October.

A state of virtual panic set in as people saw the preparations for war. The first people to go were the state and federal government officials. Records and equipment vitally important to them were packed up and hauled away, however, most of their items were left behind. After all, they were certain they would be back in a few months. They closed up their homes and packed what they needed for the temporary relocation. The people in the metropolitan area of Salt Lake City saw convoys of cars, trucks, RV's and motorcycles steadily streaming out of the cities. Even the military began moving their families out. This process started slowly, but by mid-September it was gathering steam.

Each night, footage of the migration eastward was shown on the news, both locally and nationally. The news began reporting that the rebels were committing atrocities against those leaving. These reports, however, were false. Those following the newly elected leaders in the West were instructed not to harm or hinder anyone in their exodus. We were also instructed not to disturb their homes or businesses in any way. For the most part, this order was followed. There was some theft and vandalizing which occurred during this time, but it was committed by those who were leaving. They saw this as their chance to rip off their neighbors and local businesses with impunity. They then would blame it on the rebels. The controlled media gladly reported their false claims, which were then used as additional "evidence" against the rebels, and which were also used to support the untrue accusations of the Washington government against the people in the West.

The inspired leaders in Christ's kingdom, in conjunction with the newly elected state leaders in the West, sent out a proclamation to all citizens in the areas within the western federation, which extended from Canada to Northern Mexico. They asked for calm. They reminded us that if we remained righteous and faithful, that Christ would direct us through this crisis, by his Prophets. They said that we would be protected and that we would be aided by the Priesthood of God in our defense, like unto Moses and the children of Israel against Egypt in ancient times.

The new government of Christ began a systematic organization of all able-bodied men, young and old. Inspired direction led to the creation of a defense force that centered around local priesthood leaders. The emphasis was not just on weapons, but was primarily on righteousness. These men and their families were strongly encouraged to fast and pray for the guiding and protecting hand of Christ to be with us. The highest level of obedience was required. We were asked to keep all of God's commandments-to love all (even our enemies), to be pure in heart and to stay close to the Savior. To any outsider looking on, this would have appeared wholly inadequate to prepare us for the military onslaught that was building against us outside of the mountains. They could not fathom the true power that comes from a pure Christ-like love and from righteousness.

There is a tendency for mortals to assume that only those things that can be touched and seen count for anything. If we see an army with legions of men dressed for battle, if we see huge stockpiles of guns, grenades and bullets, if we see missile systems and bombs, and if we see row upon row of tanks and planes arrayed in battle formation, we think that is power. We tremble with fear at the potential for its use against us unless we have an equally large military machine of our own. This is how the world ultimately sees power and might; indeed this is how the United States viewed its position as it prepared to conquer the West. It calculated that the western rebels with their new government were no match for the accumulated military might of the US government.

From the US military bases on the West Coast, and in the South and the Midwest, they moved their forces into place at the foothills of the mountains in New Mexico, Colorado, Wyoming, California and Oregon. They did not seal off the roads at this time because people were still pouring out of the mountains to reach the safety promised them. With the military in place by early October, it just waited to do its work until the election was over.

The Washington government had started a recruiting blitz some months back. This was done to rebuild its diminished forces. They had lost many men during the turmoil of the previous nine or ten months. The people lost were those who were loyal to the Constitution, who either left or who were killed in the purges. Now they needed to rebuild the military. The promise of jobs, excitement and plunder motivated many to join this "new" military. These recruits were not the caliber of the previous groups of men and women, but they were willing to do the President's work for a price. As this rebuilding process rapidly continued, and as the military finished positioning itself in strategic places around the West, the generals were confident of their superior position.

The military made the mistake of seeing only the power of the world. They forgot the lessons taught by ancient circumstances. They forgot about the army of Sennacherib, which was destroyed by the angel of the Lord, even as he boasted of his military might and accomplishments. They also did not understand that the same fate was prophesied to befall those who came against the people of the Lord in the latter days. They forgot how the prophet Enoch had used Priesthood power to defend a pure and righteous people in the city of Enoch. They forgot that Elisha had used the Priesthood to lead the armies of the King of Syria into captivity. Elisha's servant trembled with fear as he saw the Syrian army surrounding the town of Dothan, only to have Elisha tell him, "They that be with us are more than they that be with them..."

Then the servant's eyes were opened and he saw that the mountain was full of chariots of fire round about Elisha.

At that time, many in the West were fearful, but our prophet leaders told us not to fear, for we had the power of God with us, against which no army could stand. Indeed, they that were with us were more than they that were with them, for they had only the arm of flesh.

Despite this guidance, not every member of the Church was convinced of the power of our position. As more and more of the government people left the large cities in the West, those people who had taken the loyalty oath and received the ID chip in their hands began leaving, too. The flow out of the West was a river by the end of September. Even the weather seemed to cooperate as the winter storms held off longer than usual. Many of the members of the Church who had been reluctant to fully commit to Christ and join His kingdom, now looked on in alarm.

They had tried to keep their feet in both worlds during the rising turmoil, but they could no longer straddle the line. They had to choose. They simply could not see how the Church and kingdom of God could survive what was coming, and so they bolted and ran. By October, this group was hurriedly packing a few things, throwing them in their cars and fleeing. They grabbed their valuables, and took their children and wives. Many could not convince their wives to go. These women pleaded with their husbands to stay, telling them to trust the Lord. In the end, many of these women stayed behind with as many of their children as they could convince to stay with them. These women and children were moved by their church leaders into the places of safety.

Not all human migration at this time was out of the West. There was a steady stream of people from the East Coast, Midwest, South and West Coast who had been coming to the mountains. They had heard of Christ's kingdom. They knew that we had re-established the Constitution and that there was peace and liberty among us. They were men and women of integrity who were not willing to follow the dictatorship. Persecution against them had been accelerating for months. Over the summer, they had found that being quiet was not going to get them through. The pressure to take the ID chip and swear loyalty to the dictatorship was becoming unavoidable. They knew that if they stayed they would be required to submit or die. So they left. They went into hiding, moving as they could toward the West. This proved incredibly difficult and dangerous. Many died of exposure. If they were caught, they were tortured, raped and killed.

Vanguards of men were sent by the kingdom of God out of the mountains. These groups of men established safe corridors for the refugees to use in their migration west. These men also assisted as many as possible once they had reached the outposts of these safe corridors. Many never made it that far.

So you see, there was a two-way flow going on across the country, a separation as it were. One group was flowing out of the West. It consisted of those trying to get away from the impending military onslaught. They had either decided to accept the government's edicts under the Edmunds Initiative or they had insufficient faith that the kingdom of God could protect them; so they fled. The other group was flowing into the West. This group consisted of those who were devoutly religious and were unwilling to follow the dictatorship, or they were people who were staunch supporters of the Constitution and who liked what they saw in the new government of Christ in the West. Many who arrived said that they did not want to join the Church, but would obey our laws and would live in peace with us. This they were allowed to do. After all, religious freedom is a foundational part of the Constitution, as well as a basic tenet of the gospel of Christ. All these people, members or non-members, religious or not, were brought into our communities and were made a part of the workings of those communities. These were the honorable and good people of the earth. They helped us with our businesses, schools and political government.

As this process continued, a black cloud settled ever more firmly over all parts of the nation, except in the Mountain West. The growing evil of FEMA and the military leaders was more and more determined to drive out all who believed in Christ and the Constitution. They wanted to be free of the irritation caused by the righteous. The problem was, that as the righteous were driven out, the light of their knowledge, understanding and wisdom was lost as well. A kind of stifling darkness settled over the country from coast to coast and it became almost impossible for truth to be spoken anywhere. Only among Christ's people was there light and truth. It was sad to see how eagerly the wicked people of our once great nation now turned to the darkness. If only they had realized the terrible consequences of a life filled with darkness instead of light.

Darkness by its very nature is the absence of light. This means that darkness and light are incompatible and cannot occupy the same place at the same time. Light illuminates, it reveals and teaches the reality of all it touches. It warms and makes life possible. It shows things as they really are. Darkness hides and conceals. It can bring coldness and even death. It can create misunderstanding and deception.

People by their nature tend to gravitate toward either light or darkness. Either they choose righteousness, and the light of truth, or they choose wickedness and the darkness of evil that shrouds, distorts and destroys all that it eventually touches. As darkness shuns light, even so evil shuns righteousness. For the sake of greed, lust, pride and selfishness, evil tries to avoid the demands of truth. Evil attempts to violate and destroy truth with impunity. It mistakes pleasure for happiness, sex for love, pride for self-worth, worldly knowledge for truth, flattery for respect and forced obedience for peace. It covets a man-made world of facades, illusions and extremes, and values the appearance over substance.

Righteousness is everything evil is not. It recognizes the divine source of all it has received. It strives for substance-not show, reality-not illusion, honest self esteem-not pride, real peace-not forced obedience, happiness-not empty pleasure, truth-not deception and the pure love of Christ-not empty gratification. For all these reasons and more, righteousness and evil cannot coexist for long. Either the righteous will convert the evil with love and understanding, or the evil will drive out or destroy the righteous.

This pattern of evil has been followed for thousands of years, such as: when the armies of the wicked came against Enoch and his people; when Lot and his family were forced to leave Sodom and Gomorrah; when Alma and his people at the waters of Mormon had to flee; when Christians in the early Church were persecuted at Jerusalem; when the Saints were driven out of Missouri and Illinois; when the communists took over Russia and China in the early 1900's and killed millions. Now we witnessed the repetition of this pattern here in America as evil people struggled to justify their wickedness and gratify their lusts by turning on good people everywhere. They turned on devout Christians wherever they found them, whether they were Mormon or Baptist, Catholic or Methodist, or any member of other denominations who loved Christ. Honorable men and women everywhere became targets of government abuse.

What began as a purge of the Mormons, soon spread across the country and became a general purge of all followers of Christ; then it rippled outward to include all defenders of the Constitution, whether they were religious or not. Truly it had begun upon His house and had gone forth from there.

However, the wicked had forgotten the consequence of driving the righteous away. They had forgotten that each time they drove the righteous from among them, destruction followed. Occasionally there was a delay, but ultimately destruction always followed. Isaiah prophesied that the righteous would be taken away and then the evil would be destroyed. The wicked must have forgotten that part of the pattern, for, had it not been for the righteous among them, their destruction would have occurred earlier. Now that the separation was almost complete, there was no reason for the Lord to withhold His Almighty hand.

The Dictator President and his people were moving toward their full extent of wickedness. Like the *Book of Mormon* people of Ammonihah, who drove some of the righteous out and killed the rest, our government drove many of the righteous out; then tortured and killed the rest. The prophecies never stated that all the righteous would live through the bad times. Indeed, some died for their testimonies of Christ and His truths; they were received unto Him in glory, as was spoken of by Alma concerning the righteous people who died in Ammonihah. This great wickedness was allowed in order that God's judgments upon this evil generation of Americans, which was now ripe in iniquity, might be just. If the wicked had understood what was to follow once the righteous were gone, they might not have been so eager to drive the righteous out.

As August, September and October passed, the Dictator President called for candidates to step forward and run for office. He said it was time to elect new officials at all levels. He spoke of how things were getting better. He mentioned the coming military campaign in the West and said it would last only a few months, and then the United States would be united again. He said it was time to get our government fully organized so that it could function properly. He said those who were disloyal and traitorous will have been dealt with, and we then could go forward a better and safer country. Part of what he said was true. The country would be reunited, but not under his dictatorial government.

As candidates stepped up to register, each one had to be approved by FEMA and the military leaders. This election would not be left to chance. Each person on the register was screened. Only those who were of the same political persuasion as the President were allowed on the ballot. This was identical to the past procedure employed in Utah in the state school board races. In the end, it did not matter for whom one cast his vote, because at that time in Utah, only the Governor's people would be elected to the State School Board. In this national "election," only the President's people would be elected to each position. No more real choice, just a false election to legitimize a dictator's position.

There were plenty of people willing to fill the candidate slots. After all, there was money and power for the winners. There were campaign meetings held in each state, county and city. Each area was required to make it "look good". They wanted people to think this was legitimate. Brochures were mailed out, TV time was used, press conferences were held and the candidates went out to press the flesh. When that first Tuesday in November came, there was a good turnout for the vote. People were told it was their duty to vote. Few missed the point and voted due to fear of reprisals. No great surprises came out of this election. Each candidate who won immediately gave an acceptance speech that included praises for the President and his skillful handling of the crisis. Each one voiced approval for the Edmund's Initiative. The President also won in this election. He personally chose an unknown as his opposition; there would be no slipups.

A few days after the election, the President convened the new Congress. Due to extenuating circumstances, he said the Congress must be sworn in immediately. This was done. They ratified all of his actions forthwith and swiftly declared war on the rebels in the West. The new Congress called for the President to deal with these traitors. Much show was made of all this choreographed unity. Prearranged "spontaneous" rallies popped up in each state. The people came carrying banners praising the President and calling on him to punish the Mormons for the harm they had done to the country. The President, appearing to bow to popular demand, ordered the military to deal with the rebels.

Now the military sealed all mountain passes; roads in and out of the West. The vanguard of men sent by the government of Christ to help the refugees coming in was withdrawn back into the mountains. Salt Lake City and other western cities were now at one-fourth of their original population. Most of the people had fled. Even the US/UN military coalition troops had withdrawn. They did not want to be in harm's way during the initial missile and bombing attacks. These cities were eerie with their deserted streets. The traffic lights no longer worked. The phone system was out and electricity was spotty at best. The people remaining were primarily the righteous who had refused to go. The elected officials of the Constitutionally-based Western government went to work immediately. They organized the remaining population and put their officials in charge until new elections could be held for these cities. The main concern was to get basic services running, which they did.

The President of the Western government went to the Prophet and asked him to inquire of the Lord as to what we should do for our defense. This request actually was made weeks ago, probably in late September. The answer had been that we were to place our men at the mountain extremes, both east and west, where they would have a clear view of all that would approach from the plains and the valleys below. They were to watch the passes and the sides closely. The Lord told them that the attack would not occur until the first part of November. The most spiritual men were to be over each unit as its captain. These men were to be called and set apart by Priesthood authority to receive inspiration and revelation for their units. Groups of these captains were placed under the direction of a general, who was an inspired man as well. There were several generals who, in turn, were placed under a chief commander who was selected from among the apostles of the Church.

The men in the units were armed with all manner of guns, ammunition, grenades, mortars, rocket launchers, anti-tank guns and with those tanks and planes that were available. These had been obtained through former US military men who were sympathetic to the Constitution; they had joined us in our defense of freedom. Even so, our military hardware was definitely numerically inferior to the weaponry of the US/UN forces.

However, our military leaders were righteous men who wore the armor of God. The Lord told the men that if they would be faithful in all things, humbling themselves before Him, He would guide and help them as He did Gideon of old. The Lord revealed to our military leaders the strategy of attack of our enemies. We were told to fast and pray in preparation, as the city of Enoch did. All citizens of the West declared a day of fasting, and prayed continually for the help and guidance of the Lord in this crisis. As a result of the humility of the people, the Lord revealed to our leaders what they should do.

As we waited for the first movements of ground troops from the other side, a series of strategies were put into place by our forces. We had ground to air missiles that would take out a plane. These were located at the places where it was revealed that the planes would fly in. Additionally, the Lord told them to use the Priesthood to turn back the missiles. Now our forces were ready to repel the attackers. We were specifically forbidden to attack our enemy first. We were told to act in defense only. No needless killing was to occur, or we would lose the blessings of heaven. This command was obeyed. Now our troops waited in silence for the enemy to move first.

On the other side, ground troops were positioned at the major freeway points into and out of the West. It was assumed that these were the logical places to move large numbers of men into the mountains. The US/UN troops were very confident of their position, so much so that they grew careless. Normal precautions and attention to detail were ignored; the assumption was that brute force would easily win. Government leaders watched as their ranks grew daily with the arrival of new recruits. The recruitment blitz by Washington had paid off handsomely; the US military leaders now felt so confident of their position that they allowed the UN troops to pull back. They said that they could handle it alone.

They did not notice that those UN military units that had loyalties to Russia and China had already quietly withdrawn. These units moved back to predetermined bases along the coasts. These bases were near strategically positioned seaports and large airfields along the east and west coasts. Looking back, it was so obvious what these forces were doing, that it is amazing that the US military and political leaders in Washington, D.C. did not catch it. They were so intent on crushing us that they did not watch their back door.

The day of the attack arrived. It was the middle of November. The enemy forces had a series of air campaigns planned for starters. We had been forewarned and were waiting. Some of our western leaders had prepared powerful jamming devices that created confusion in the jet communications systems. As the first raids of jets came up toward the mountains, these electronic devices were turned on. They worked better than we had hoped. Confusion resulted and our men on the ground fired many ground-to-air missiles that locked onto the heat source from the jets. Almost all the jets were shot down or forced to retreat. The loss in planes was enormous. Repeated waves of jets were sent in from California, Colorado and Wyoming. This went on for several days with no success.

Next came the missiles. These also were expected and were turned back, this time by use of the Priesthood. As missile after missile came overhead, units of Priesthood bearers were watching and would repel the missiles by righteous command. The missiles either turned back to where they came from, or fell into the mountain peaks below them where their explosions did no harm. This combined air and missile assault went on for days, but to no avail. The generals of our enemies were frustrated. They felt there was a traitor among them who was telling the defenders where the next attack would be. Such was not the case. The defenders had prophet leaders guiding them, much as Elisha guided the Israelite armies of old.

Next came the ground assault. Large columns of helicopters, personnel carriers, tanks, trucks and other vehicles moved out. From the west, these units embarked from the Victorville and Reno areas. From the east, they began in the Amarillo, Denver and Casper areas. Each convoy was miles long. The western defense plan was to let these columns advance to predetermined locations where an appropriate plan awaited each group. No one plan was the same as each convoy had its own unique make-up of machinery and men. The Lord had revealed these plans to the leaders of the defense force for the west. The captains of each unit told their men that if they would show the courage of Gideon's men and the faith and righteousness of the Sons of Helaman, that the Lord would protect them and bless them with success. A flag was made with the words of the "Title of Liberty" upon it; it was raised over each unit. This became their motto. At Thanksgiving time, when all should have been home enjoying a feast of gratitude, our men were fighting a battle for our freedom and our lives, right here in the West. It was hard to believe that it was only one year ago that the economic collapse had occurred, which had started all of these happenings.

It took about a week for these convoys to get into place and prepare their base camps. Then they felt they could fan out over the Mountain West and start their operation of genocide. At that point the traps were sprung, each trap being different. All the traps were initiated on the same day so as to prevent the enemy from being able to warn one another. The sudden and intense nature of our attack caused each military column to be pinned down in those predetermined locations chosen by our defense leaders. Each trap was designed to create confusion within the ranks of the enemy units. The element of surprise, along with the appropriate and cleverly timed use of planes, tanks, rockets and hidden gunmen, created the illusion of the defenders being much more numerous than previously thought. Indeed, it also created the feeling that the attackers were already in the midst of the enemy ranks. There were explosions, fires, billowing smoke and gunfire everywhere. Defending troops were waiting with anti-tank and ground-to-air missiles. Any attempt to move a tank would result in that tank being blown up. Any attempt to use a helicopter would lead to it being shot down. The tank and helicopter crews soon fled in terror and the ground forces themselves turned on one another, not knowing who their enemies were.

The mayhem that followed was so great that the military ranks broke down; the US troops began a retreat in utter confusion. Our men were already stationed along the way and continued firing on any vehicle, tank or helicopter that attempted to move. The lead ones were especially targeted. This left the road out strewn with military hardware, some of it destroyed, much of it abandoned. Our forces quickly moved in and took all the tanks, helicopters and vehicles that were salvageable. We had been informed that they would be needed later.

Any retreating troops were left unmolested as long as they continued to leave. We were strictly forbidden to commit the wanton shedding of blood. In each case of retreat or surrender, we were to save every life possible. However, rather than a retreat, it was more like a rout. Many of the enemy leaders had been killed in the battles, and the enlisted men were mostly inexperienced. Most of them were the new recruits who had joined for some excitement and plunder. They were not expecting to be shot at, much less attacked in earnest. When the surprise attacks occurred, they were caught completely off guard and reacted with confused self-interest. There was little military discipline among them. Such discipline would have been needed to coordinate a response. It was phenomenal that a few righteous men had sent thousands fleeing.

Word spread quickly of the horrible defeat the enemy troops had suffered. There was great celebration in the cities of the West; a day of fasting and prayer was declared to give thanks to the Lord for His protecting care. It was the first part of December. The entire campaign had lasted a mere three-and-a-half weeks. However, we did not put down our guard.

In Washington, D.C. the President called in the surviving military leaders and asked them what had happened. One by one they gave their accounts. Each said they were caught off guard and now knew what needed to be done to achieve success. The President seemed to listen sympathetically and then suggested an alternative. At that point, a military guard came in. He arrested all of the leaders who had failed, and took them away. They were removed in the presence of a group of younger officers of lower rank. These young officers were immediately elevated to the leading positions within the military. They were escorted outside where they watched as each failed leader was executed by a firing squad. The point was not lost on them. The President then sternly warned them that he expected that they would not let him down. He said he wanted a new offensive against the West prepared. It would never occur, and he would not live to see what happened next. The President's actions over the last year had driven the military's best men out of the service, or had killed them. This would prove to be a great tragedy, since the military would desperately need such experience very soon.

While we were fighting a civil war here at home, the Russian, Chinese, Islamic alliance was doing all it could to bottle up affairs at the UN in New York. It was continually throwing accusations at the U.S. and it's allies for this or that offense, real or imagined. The leader of this alliance positioned himself as a savior from the world's troubles. More and more his advice seemed good. At the same time, the militaries of these countries were working together for a coordinated attack on the United States, Europe and the Middle East. First, the United States of America had to be taken out. This alliance was looking on hungrily as we fought among ourselves. They could almost taste success as we so easily let them position their troops on our coasts by our major seaports and airfields. The leaders of the alliance called several meetings, and promised that their individual desires would be met if they would just be patient a little longer. A plan was set for China to seize Taiwan in mid December and annex it. This would be the catalyst for the invasion. They knew that America and Western Europe would object. Before either group could react, however, they would launch an organized attack on the U.S. and Western Europe in the name of protecting their sovereignty. Then they would seize the wealth of both areas to pay the cost of the war.

The plan was to conquer the land of the United States. There was no intention of saving the population. They did not want to rule over the people. They wanted all of the people disposed of so that they could have the wealth and natural resources for themselves. This was to be a wholesale slaughter of the entire population of the United States of America. The plan in Western Europe was to conquer the land and the people. They would enslave the population and use it to run their factories and businesses. They would also use their knowledge and technology. The whole plan seemed so ideal. They were so caught up in it that they failed to give any real notice to what was occurring in the Mountain West of the United States. That proved to be a major miscalculation.

There were a few more things of interest that were occurring. The harvest for the United States was not very good. It was well below normal, which left food supplies extremely tight. Remember, due to all the upheaval, the crop was not planted on time or in the usual quantity. The food distribution system of the United States had also been impaired. Rationing was conducted on a national basis. Starvation, however, was not the major problem it had been the previous winter, during the riots. In the West, the situation was improving but food was still tight. The harvest was better but there were proportionately more mouths to feed.

The Washington government encountered another problem. They had intentionally encouraged all the "loyal citizens" in the West to leave. They had assured them that the war against the rebels would be short, and that all these loyal supporters would be able to go home soon. Now with their defeat, these people who had left their homes in the West could not go back. They were stranded in temporary camps that had been set up for them. No provision had been made to take care of them long term, and winter was now upon them. These people were unprepared for survival in this harsh environment. In their rush to get out of the Mountain West, they had not taken the supplies, equipment and clothing necessary for life in such camps. They had few cooking pots or utensils. Many left without coats or boots. There were few sleeping bags and blankets, certainly not enough to keep the people warm.

Unrest soon surfaced in the camps as people began dying of exposure and starvation. The military that was supposed to protect them, viciously turned on them as it suppressed their demonstrations. These citizens found themselves prisoners in the "safe camps," while a distant government ignored its promises to them. Many now looked longingly to the West that they had recently abandoned. They wondered if they would ever see their homes again. The vast majority never would. As circumstances evolved, these people were later driven in death marches to the east, after the foreign invasion started. It was expected that they could help fight, or at the very least, block a few bullets. They became a pitiful example of how worldly governments deal with their citizens.

In the West, as the kingdom of Christ steadily grew, several large caches of ancient records were revealed. These had been hidden for centuries, in some cases, millennia. They represented huge, ancient libraries that had been stored away in the depths of the Mountain West. Some came from the mountains proper. Others came from the canyon country to the south. Yet others came from the regions of central and southern Mexico. The records were rapidly and quietly transferred to the central areas of the kingdom of Christ. There they were stored in a few of the temples that had been prepared for this purpose. Along with these records were discovered several Urim and Thummim. These were tools of translation of ancient languages. The Lord designated several people to prepare themselves to translate these records. The books were primarily written on metal plates, and represented several languages. It was a marvel to us all. As the first translated information became available, it opened our eyes to amazing new ideas and ways of perceiving life.

CHAPTER 9

MY FAMILY

Before I go on, I really need to take just a few moments and tell how all these events affected my family directly. I will make it short.

Shortly after the crisis began, our home was damaged in the two earthquakes. We managed to get it fixed up enough to make it livable. Anna and I were fortunate that we had a large extended family, lots of friends and the Church. It also helped that I had contacts through my business. With all this, we got back on our feet quickly. But with the collapsed economy, our income was only a tiny fraction of what it was previously. It took all I earned to just cover our house payment. We actually had to start using our food storage. Imagine that. I guess we thought that day would never come. Then Anna's brother, Alex, lost his job. She came to me with a cloud of worry on her face.

"Clay, can we let Alex and his family stay here? Their home is being foreclosed on. They have nowhere else to go." There was pleading in her eyes.

"What about your parent's home?" I asked.

"It was too badly damaged in the earthquake. They are not even sure if they can stay there. And the rest of my family's homes are too small for six more people. Only our home is large enough. We can't leave them out on the street." She was almost in tears by now.

She was right. We had to help.

"Okay, they can come and stay," I said.

I have to admit I was not thrilled about this new development, but they did need our help. So they came and it turned out all right. Actually, Alex started helping me at my business, and he did fixing up around the house and the neighborhood. He was good at it, too. His wife, Samantha, (or Sam as we called her), helped Anna. The hardest part was getting used to little kids again. Their four children were much younger than ours, but that was okay. It only took awhile, and we loved them almost like our own.

Then, in December, the missionaries were all called home. Robert came back. He had not been out quite a year at that point; I noticed such a difference in him. He was much more mature and spiritual. His level of commitment to the Gospel had grown, due to serving the Lord. His perspective on life was very clear. This proved to be an inspiration and strength to all of us. Robert, now just 20 years of age, was the first to see the big trouble coming from Washington, D.C. He told Anna and me that the changes occurring in our nation's capitol would soon move like a terrible storm westward across the country, and would settle in Utah. He was right. By the beginning of March, when our governor instituted the Edmund's Initiative in Utah, his words proved to be true.

When the confusion began among some of the local leaders of the Church, some friends called us. Their bishop was asking them to turn in their food and guns. Our bishop had told us how he had been approached by the FEMA people. He explained their veiled threats and said he had prayed and fasted and felt he should refuse to comply with the order. We told those friends what our bishop had told us. They were being pressured in their area to comply with these requests. They ended up giving their food and guns to FEMA. At this point, several general authorities came out in favor of the Initiative. This caused concern among the members. People in our ward congregated at one another's homes and talked about what it all meant. Some even said they were disappointed that the Prophet had not spoken more openly about all this before it happened. I tried to gently remind them that we had been forewarned and had received guidance. Robert was more forthright; he told them that to criticize the Prophet was the first step to apostasy, and in so many words, told them to repent. You can imagine how well that was received. We were greatly relieved when the Prophet reaffirmed his rejection of the Edmunds Initiative. We were also relieved when the apostate general authorities were released. It helped clarify the Church's stand. We were still concerned to hear some of our neighbors grumbling about the Church.

In late April, our friends who had earlier called about the food and guns, showed up at our door late one night. There they stood, ten of them, four adults and six kids. We were thunderstruck.

As they stood there in the dark, cold street, I heard myself saying, "Come in, come in. What's happened? Why are you here?"

One of the fathers answered, "We turned in our food and guns. Remember that conversation we had a few weeks back? Well, we went to get some of our food and they wouldn't give it to us, not unless we swore an oath of loyalty to the President."

I could not believe my ears. Anna and I just looked at each other for a few shocked moments. Then Anna asked, "They won't let you have your own food?! What about your children? Didn't they have any compassion?" She was getting angry as she spoke. I could hear it in her voice.

I said, "Anna, let them answer one question at a time. They've obviously been through a lot." Turning back to the father I said, "Tell us more about what happened."

He went on, "Well, we knew we couldn't take such an oath since the President is such a bad man. Because of that, no food was forthcoming . Then, when we left, we were followed. After we got home one of our neighbors warned us that he'd overheard them say that they would be back to arrest us, that they would teach us for not cooperating. We grabbed our kids and piled into our cars and came here. We didn't know where else to go." Now his shoulders drooped and his eyes had a look of pleading like I had never seen before. He truly was desperate, and afraid. Anna picked right up on that.

"Of course you can stay here. We have plenty of food. It might be a little tight, but we'll make do. Besides, we can all help each other." She was beside herself with eagerness to help these people. As I looked at Anna, my heart swelled with appreciation for the good, Christ-like woman that she was.

I said, "Well, let's find sleeping accommodations for everyone. It is late and I'll bet you're tired."

We finally had everyone in bed. Anna and I could hardly sleep. It was becoming apparent that these FEMA and military people were dangerous and this Initiative (as it was so politely called) was destructive. We talked late into the night. We were amazed at our governor's involvement in all this. We were concerned that some members were being sucked in by it. We wondered what would come next.

The morning sun found our home filled to capacity. The reality of the previous night now became a functional problem. Fixing food for 21 people was a major event, but the women all pitched in and the work went along well. It was amazing how well the different talents of the people came into play to meet our needs. The men helped Alex and me with my work, and they found any odd jobs they could to raise a little extra cash or to obtain barter items. There were conflicts from time to time, but these were dealt with individually or in a multifamily council.

In this manner, these conflicts were resolved as soon as they arose so that they would not become major. It was surprising how well we got along. As I looked up and down my street, it was soon apparent that we were not the only home with several families in it. By the end of April, many of the houses had two or three families in them. The large numbers of people in each house created practical problems that we resolved in creative ways. Each couple was assigned a bedroom where they would sleep along with their younger children. All the older boys were combined and slept together in the game room. The older girls were also combined, and they slept together in the family room. One washing machine and dryer made it necessary to require everyone to wear their clothes three days at a time. This reduced the use of the machine to a livable level. Most clothes were dried on a clothesline. Drinking and cooking water still had to be boiled. This became a time-consuming job for the older kids. The adults took turns working together to keep the kids' education going. We had a makeshift school functioning that soon grew to involve much of the neighborhood. Different subjects were taught by different people on the block according to their separate abilities. We were surprised to find that we could address all of the subjects within a four-hour period each morning. This was possible because we just taught basics, no social extras. This left the afternoons free for the children to play or do their chores. The ward continued functioning very well and, if anything, became more cohesive as we stretched out to help others around us who were in need.

It is said that the only constant is change, and that seemed to be the order of the day back then. Anna came to my office one day in mid-May; she was excited and concerned.

"Clay, our bishop just called a special meeting. He says that the Prophet has given some direction that he wants all of us to hear."

I asked, "When is the meeting?"

"It is at the chapel tonight at seven p.m.", she answered.

So we went to the meeting. We were told that the Lord had directed that the faithful Saints were to gather to specific areas for safety. Many of these areas already had towns on site that would now be expanded. Other areas were essentially undeveloped, but were to be built into towns and cities. If we were already in a designated safe area, we were to organize ourselves and prepare to receive those who would come. If we were in an area where we would have to evacuate, we were to be organized for that migration by ward and stake. This was to be done under the direction of the area authorities who would be guided by the Prophet as he received revelation from the Savior. All was to be done in order. No one was to go until directed. Committees were to be appointed that would prepare necessities like travel plans and supplies, building materials, food supplies, education, entertainment, health needs, utilities, etc. The plan was carefully thought out. A force was also organized for security. Calls, much like mission calls, went out inviting each member to accept work in their own areas.

Robert came to me, "Dad, I have been asked to serve in the security force. We'll also help with transportation, at least at first. I'll need some food supplies to take with me and some camping gear. I hope that is okay with you."

I guess I did not expect him to be called on so soon, but I was pleased at his willingness to help. Companies of such men were being assembled. Robert's group was comprised of younger men like himself. Their leader was an acquaintance of mine who had served in the Church in our area. He was one of the most spiritual men I knew. As I looked at him at the head of this throng of 20-year-olds, I could not help but think of Helaman and his 2,000 stripling warriors. Nostalgia aside, we loaded Robert up and gave him as much food as he could carry; we extracted a promise from him that he would write often. He was to be heavily involved in this work for the next year. Nevertheless, we did see him occasionally. Each time I saw him he was more of a man, with all the qualities a father would hope to see in a son.

We were not asked to move at first, so we took care of the needs of daily life for several months. During those months, things got worse in the big cities to the north of us. Troop movements for the President's military became more bold and intrusive. Bombings and general resistance escalated, too. It seemed like the more the President's people tightened their grip, the more the population fought back. With each bombing or attack against the military, there were more arrests and reprisals. We became aware of the trouble through our family and friends.

My brother Tim called. He said, "The PDF and the military raided a construction company in Sandy. They said they were aiding the rebels. They shot the owner, arrested all of his employees and loaded them into trucks and took them away. No trial, no judge. They made sure it was filmed for the evening news. Clay, the owner was a friend of mine. I know that he was not involved in any bombings or assistance with the rebels. There is no justice anymore."

I said, "Tim, some of my local friends tell me that the same kinds of things are happening down here. Apparently, a few days ago a group of the PDF went through some homes in the Orem area. They had no search warrants. They simply said they had heard that the people in that area were not loyal to the President, and that was justification enough for them to punish them. They took the people outside of each home and demanded that they take an oath of loyalty to the President. Everyone who refused was killed on the spot. They tore the houses apart and took anything of value they wanted, especially the food."

There were a few moments of silence, then Tim said, "If we are to be safe at all, we'll either have to knuckle under and join these goons the President has sent, or we're all going to have to leave these cities. They simply aren't safe anymore. I hear of more and more people who just disappear or who are arrested without cause. Once they're in the hands of these FEMA people and their goons, they are as good as dead. None of them ever comes back."

These kinds of stories were abundant, and the evidence of their truthfulness was everywhere. But the news was not all bad. At the end of May the announcement was made that the political kingdom of Christ was forming. One night after work, Anna told me that our home teachers had come by. They had brought a flier that explained that the government of Christ was beginning to operate. Christ would now serve as our king, judge and lawgiver. The flier explained that Christ had personally met with a number of people, His organization was currently being filled with righteous men and women. They would serve as the core group upon which the rest of the government would be built. The vast majority of those selected were members of the Church, although a few were not. Anna by now was politically active, and so we were not too surprised when one of her political friends came by with some interesting news. His name was Dale.

"Anna, Clay, you'll never guess what has happened."

"You've been selected to be part of the new government", said Anna. She was half kidding when she said it. After all, that would be almost too good to be true.

He responded, "Yes! Isn't it wonderful. I'm so excited I can hardly believe my ears. I've been asked to bring my family and move to one of the cities of refuge where the new government will be temporarily housed. It will be a lot of work, and I am concerned about my worthiness to serve."

I could not resist asking, "Do you think you'll get to meet the Savior?"

He answered, "Well ... I hope so. Yes, I guess. It would seem logical. After all, the prophesies indicate He will lead us, and how can He do that without coming to us, at least once in awhile. I know this isn't his Second Coming, but probably one of the preparatory visits spoken of."

We were to find out later that indeed Christ did meet with Dale and the others who were called. He revealed his government organization to them, and immediately sent them out to organize it in the cities of refuge that were already starting. Anna was to play a role in this later. The security forces, of which Robert was a part, were also organized under His government. They were instructed to protect all who were moving to the cities of refuge. They were also to form a defense around all areas designated by the Savior. They were not to be aggressive in any way, but were to act only in defense. A command structure was solidified and specific strategies were given. Then in late June, the bishop of our ward called Anna and I in.

"Brother and Sister Freeman ... I mean Clay, Anna. Our ward has been asked to move to an area of safety about 250 miles from here. Will you and your family support us in this?"

We hesitated only a second. I was taken aback by his forthright and blunt manner. A quick glance from Anna indicated her acceptance. "Yes, we'll go. We do need to talk to our family about this, but I am sure that they will support you, too."

The bishop continued, "We are to leave in two weeks. Committees are being organized to see to everyone's needs. Will you serve on one of these committees?"

We both agreed. I was to serve on the transportation committee and Anna was to serve on the food committee. Other committees were created to deal with shelter, housing at the new site, business, farming, etc.. It was quite involved, but a well laid out plan had been given to our bishop by the area authority over our stake. Nothing was left to chance. Obviously, there would be a lot of cross over work as time went on.

Our time to move finally arrived, and it was none too soon. The UN troops had moved into Salt Lake City and were beginning a systematic sweep through the city to enforce the Initiative. Reports of their brutality and cruelty were even worse than the ones we had previously received. They expanded their reach south and north as time allowed more of them to come into the Wasatch Front area. The Church moved rapidly to remove its records and people out, ahead of their atrocities. It had already moved all those who were willing out of the big cities into the safe areas. Those who were reluctant to move now found themselves trapped in a terrible situation. The time to leave was when the call from the Prophet came. They would now pay the price for their disobedience. As for our ward, we were out of the reach of these troops and, indeed, would be long gone before they might even get this far.

I came home a few days before we were to leave, and found Anna sitting on our porch, her face very solemn.

"What's wrong? You look like you don't have a friend in the world."

She looked up, her eyes filled with tears, and said, "Clay, we are leaving behind so much. Our work, our nice things, our memories. There is so much we simply can't take. Oh, I know we'll be okay. We can get by with a lot less than we are used to. Still, it's so hard."

I sat and held her close. It occurred to me that conversations like this probably occurred in Nauvoo as the Saints prepared to leave their homes. At least we had trucks and trailers to move us. We had carefully saved our gasoline and other fuels. We would be all right. We were not moving in the dead of winter, and the distance was not bad, even if we had to walk. However, the sacrifice was great. The time to fulfill the covenants we had made had finally arrived, and promises to sacrifice all for the kingdom of God now had very real meaning. Only a portion of the ward actually agreed to do what was asked. It was a little surprising to see who went and who stayed. Not all of the "active" families decided to go. Among those who did go were people who might previously have been considered "inactive." When push came to shove, there were some who stepped forward and surprised us.

It was the first part of July. The day to leave arrived and an odd caravan of cars, trucks, vans, and SUVs congregated at the chapel. Many were pulling trailers. All were loaded to the top. Comfort definitely was not the order of the day as every available space was filled with something. We even had equipment for repair of vehicles on the road. Speed was not the issue; safety was a greater concern. An escort was provided for us by the new security force. We were delighted to see our son in that group. It was heartwarming to be with him again, even if it was only for a day or two. Kayla and Deanna lavished him with attention, which you could tell he liked, and they could not help teasing him a little, too.

The whole trip only took a day. We arrived at a remote valley. It was bound on one side by high mountains, and on the other by a canyon. The area was beautiful; the accommodations were spartan but adequate. We established a ward camp. There were other wards coming in and all had been assigned a place for their tents. Our camp was set up by nightfall, and food was prepared.

We learned the next day that large quantities of a new type of temporary building material had been brought in. This was available for our use in building dwelling structures for our families until more permanent homes could be constructed. These materials were a pre-fab, lightweight wall that could be combined in different ways to make large or small structures. These structures were insulated, watertight, and could be heated in winter. However, there was no air conditioning or indoor plumbing, as of yet. Large, nice public restrooms had been prepared before our arrival. Obviously, a lot of thought had gone into this project. Within a few weeks we had all of our families out of their tents and into these solid "temporary shelters." These were to be our homes for awhile until we could build more traditional homes later. At that time, these would serve as storage sheds or garages.

We all planted gardens immediately. Businesses, churches, farms, and schools were started as well. This refuge now was a rapidly growing city of thousands. We were met by representatives of the new government of Christ. They explained His plan and asked for a sustaining vote, which they received. We were organized according to His plan. Because of our previous political involvement, Anna and I were asked to participate as delegates to the Constitutional Convention that was to be held in late July. This we agreed to do. The whole process was a lot of work, but was well worth it.

We were told that this same kind of thing was happening throughout the western mountains and was expanding almost daily. We also met people coming and going from other cities of refuge. They had stories to tell that thrilled us. To our surprise, we met many Indians who were building their own cities of refuge within Christ's kingdom. They, too, were serving as leaders in the government of Christ and often came to meet with us and instruct us. Old animosities and prejudices melted away as these two branches of the House of Israel worked together and became one in the hand of the Savior.

Our temporary home was little more than four walls with a roof, door and two windows. The beds were in one end, and the cooking facilities and dinner table were in the other end. We hung curtains at night to gain some privacy, but it was minimal. At least we were not sharing our home anymore, though we kind of missed the closeness.

Then, at the end of July, Anna and I went to the main city where the government of Christ was centered. It was built around a temple. We were told that this would remain as the center until we went back to Independence, Missouri, to build the New Jerusalem. A meeting place had already been selected. We arrived to find delegates from all over the western US, Canada and Mexico. Each delegate represented cities or areas of refuge. Because of that, the Indian peoples were heavily represented at that convention.

The meeting was opened and rules of conduct established. The Constitutional Convention agreed that our purpose was to re-establish the Constitution in its original form. This was discussed for several days. Proposals were made. All was done in an attitude of prayer and righteous desire. The collective result was the re-establishment of our beautiful Constitution. All the dross was removed. This refined and renewed Constitution was then presented to the Savior for His approval, which He gave.

Immediately, copies were made of the document and it was sent throughout the West. Copies were also sent out to the world, especially to the areas of the United States still under the Dictator President's control. Suffice it to say, all the areas of refuge, city by city and state by state, ratified the document. It was as if a monstrous weight had been lifted off our shoulders. No more meddling government bureaucrats. No more high taxes. No more regulations from unelected officials. No more restrictions on religious freedom in the deceptive name of separation of church and state. From north to south, the breath of freedom was almost audible. The gasp of alarm in Washington, D.C. and Salt Lake City was almost as audible.

At this time, we went back to our separate cities of refuge to work at our businesses, homes and farms. The gold in the mountains was now opened up in huge abundance, and a new monetary system was created. It was based on gold and silver coin. All dollars in the western areas were bought out by the new treasury department. Within a four-week period all commerce was functioning within this new system. We were surprised to learn how many countries around the world quickly and quietly approached the government of Christ to establish trade based on this new monetary system. Centers were established where goods produced could be exchanged for gold or silver. In addition, these same goods could then be purchased for personal use or resale. These centers came to function as a type of warehouse/bank distribution system. All excess production was funneled through the local bishops, who then used it to help other people get started in education, business, homes or work. Large community projects were funded in a similar way. Debt as we know it vanished since the new system was equity based, not debt based.

I started my business back up and was able to bring in supplies to sell for people to use. Our temporary home was okay, but Anna wanted something more permanent, so we made plans for a house to be built on our lot. We started the footings for it by September, but it would be a long time before it would be finished. There was so much to do.

By now, most people were getting around on foot, by bicycle or horse-drawn wagons. The little gasoline and diesel fuel that was available was saved for use in long-distance trade between the cities or for the defense force. However, at this time, a new power generation system was developed that would revolutionize the way electricity was generated. This system consisted of devices that were located on site that produced all the power a home, building or project would need. It functioned by using the flow of subatomic particles through the universe to generate an endless flow of electrons. Therefore, these devices essentially contained their fuel within themselves in an unlimited supply, and produced no pollution. This system negated the need for power lines and generating plants. With time, we also found that these devices (usually black boxes of varying size depending on the need) could be mounted in vehicles to provide the fuel to drive cars, planes, trucks and tractors. All these modes of transportation were to be converted over to this fuel system. We anticipate that in time all our energy needs will be supplied by this system of power generation, which will be pollution-free. We could produce power for a tiny fraction of the previous costs. It would take sometime to convert over to this system, but we were making progress. All the cities of Zion, beginning with the center place of the New Jerusalem, would eventually be powered by this system.

One day, I was at my work when Alex and his brother came by. They had moved with us to this city and lived nearby. He had a copy of the local weekly newspaper in his hand.

"Clay, you should see this. The Dictator in D.C. is accusing us of causing all the evil that he actually caused. He is blaming us. Can you imagine that?" Alex was obviously agitated.

"May I see that?" I asked. I quickly read the article. It was as Alex said, and there was more. The Dictator was talking of attacking us. By now, we all called the President back in Washington, D.C. the "Dictator", because that is what he was.

Alex asked, "What will we do? Our defense force is no match for the U.S. military."

I said, "Don't worry. The Lord has protected his people against such odds in the past. He will do it again. You'll see. We just need to trust the Lord and have faith." Somehow, I knew that what I said was true. I was even surprised at the peaceful, calm feeling I had. I knew that all would be well.

News of this new development spread rapidly throughout the mountains. Anna and I were not surprised to find that the leaders of the new government defense force were already preparing for this attack. A call went out asking all our young and middle-aged men to join the defense force. A few older men were left behind to do the work which the others could not manage. The women and children helped in that work as much as they could.

I was sent to be with one of the units that was to defend our southeastern approach to the Mountain West. I was surprised to find out how much weaponry the defense force had accumulated. It was much more than I had expected. We had brought our own guns and what little ammunition we had, but it was small compared to what I saw when I arrived at our base camp of operations. Apparently, there had been a large number of U.S. military people who had come over to our side within the last months. When the Dictator had started his purge and seized power in the country, these men remained loyal to the Constitution, and hence, joined us. They brought with them as much military hardware as they could. They willingly volunteered to serve to defend the Constitution under the direction of the restored government.

By early September, our defense force was gathering in large numbers at all access areas to the West, both on our eastern and our western flank. We had a lot of training to do within a short period. Our chief commander over all of the military operations, was an apostle. He, along with the president of the western government, had gone to the Prophet and asked the Prophet to inquire of the Lord what we should do. The Lord answered their prayers. We were told that the attack would not occur until the first part of November, and instructions of military placement were given. These instructions were followed. We prepared and practiced, saving our ammunition until it was actually needed.

At this time, we learned that an alliance had been established between Russia, China and the Islamic States. We knew this would lead to no good. They held a summit which had all the trappings of trouble. It seemed obvious to us in the West that big trouble was brewing, but the Dictator and his followers missed it. They were so preoccupied with us that they did not see the danger behind them. They were too busy trying to consolidate their power.

I served in the campaign in Southern Colorado and Northern New Mexico. When the attack came in the middle of November, we were as ready as possible. Most important of all, a call had gone out from Church and political leaders for all citizens to fast and pray for the Lord's protection and guidance. Anna later told me how the people back in our city had fasted and prayed. Indeed, the men in my unit did the same. We knew that if we were to survive, we would need the Lord's help. The government attack was defeated by early December. The most remarkable thing about the campaign was the high spiritual caliber of our fighting men, especially our leaders. Our unit was lead by a man who was as good a man as I had ever met. He exhibited the Christ-like qualities of patience, courage, firmness in truth and gentleness. When the battle was over, our unit had a day of fasting and prayer just to say thanks to the Lord. This occurred throughout the West.

House Upon The Sand

CHAPTER 10

INVASION

S urprise reigned as news spread of how the western insurrection had defeated the U.S. military. The news caused words of derision at the UN in New York City. The mighty United States of America could not even handle an insurrection within its own boundaries. The leader of the Alliance was much more careful in his public comments. The planned invasion of the United States was only days away, and he did not want anything to ruin his plans. He still spoke sympathetically of the problems the Dictator in Washington, D.C. was having. Then, in the next breath, he would rail on the western nations for their meddling policies of the past. He said these policies would no longer be tolerated by the nations of the world. The ambassadors of Russia, China and the Islamic countries kept the UN in turmoil. Nothing substantial was accomplished.

We learned later that the Alliance had arranged for a team of assassins to enter the United States and Western Europe. Their purpose was to target those people who would be a problem for them when the international war started. At the top of the list was the Dictator President in Washington, D.C. Also, on the list were the members of the secret group of wealthy men who were trying to control the nations of the earth. In the past, the leaders of the Alliance had benefited greatly from the secret, and not so secret, help they had received from these evil men. Indeed many of these political leaders owed their current positions of power to the men in the secret organization. However, as is characteristic of such people, just as they plot against others outside of their organization, they also plot against each other within their organization. These wealthy men had hoped to use the leaders of the Alliance to do their bidding. Instead, the Alliance leaders figured that they could run the secret organization themselves.

In mid-December, the Dictator President was killed! He was gunned down in Washington, D.C. Utter confusion followed as people jockeyed for position. Technically, the vice-president should have filled the vacancy; however; he was a weak and powerless man. He had been chosen because the Dictator did not want a threat so close to him. FEMA and the new military leaders met with the vice-president and Mr. Edmunds to decide what to do. The final agreement of the meeting was that Mr. Edmunds would run the presidency from behind the scenes with the vice-president following his orders. This arrangement would continue until something more permanent could be devised. Mr. Edmunds had the backing of the military along with most of the people in FEMA. This gave him the leverage to run the country. He also arranged to have himself put in as the new vice-president. That should have made the new president very nervous.

In the West, we watched all these maneuverings with great sadness. Then our Prophet received a revelation that on Christmas Day an invasion of the country by foreign powers would take place. It would begin with a missile attack from overseas. It would include both nuclear and biological warheads. We were instructed to go into our homes and stay there for two weeks. We were told that we were not to come outside for any reason, neither were we to open our doors or windows. We were told to store within each home everything we would need to get us through that two-week period of time. Things like food, water, sanitation facilities and medicine were recommended. The members of our defense force were sent back to their homes. We were told that it was important for husbands to be with their families at this time. Single men were sent home to their families as well. All who did not have families were invited into the homes of others.

I was glad to be home, and it was equally good to have Robert home. He brought two young men with him who did not have anywhere else to go, and so they stayed with us. By the time this revelation was given, only one week remained until Christmas. It was a very busy time as people tried to get ready. In many cases, extended families combined in larger homes in order to help each other. We tried hard to be sure everyone was included. We were informed that after the two week period, that we would be able to go outdoors again for limited times. There would be parts of each day when it would be safe to go outside. This would be the case for at least two months.

Five days before Christmas, on the 20th of December, China invaded Taiwan. China declared that it was annexing Taiwan. The whole invasion was quick. The Taiwanese knew that resistance was futile; they also knew that the United States could not help them. The leaders of the western nations called an emergency session of the UN Security Council to discuss this event. As the nations gathered, there were accusations and counter-accusations. The United States and Western Europe demanded that China withdraw from Taiwan. China refused. Russia supported China, as did the other members of the Alliance.

The NATO countries called an emergency session of their own to determine how to respond to this violation of the international status quo. It was determined that military ships would be sent to the waters of Taiwan. China's financial transactions were frozen, and NATO ambassadors were called home to determine what to do, but, diplomatic ties were not severed. However, this was the only response by NATO.

The members of the Alliance were more aggressive. They all called their ambassadors and staff home. This happened the day following China's invasion. In hindsight, it is obvious they were prepared for this Taiwan thing. The Alliance countries said they were not severing diplomatic ties, only considering their situation. That was a lame announcement, but desperate people and nations tend to believe those words which will serve their own purposes, whether or not they are true. The leaders of the United States did not want to believe a war was imminent, so they overlooked the obvious. This type of thinking rendered the Washington leaders gullible to other deceptions. Prior to the attack on the West, the Alliance portion of the UN troops had withdrawn to our east and west coasts. Americans in general were not aware this had happened, and our own leaders winked at it, choosing to believe there was no reason for concern. These troops had already been on our soil for so long that the government trusted them. That was a mistake. They were setting a trap.

The next part of the Alliance's plan kicked in. A few days before Christmas, the remaining assassins killed most of the wealthy men in the secret organization. They also killed important political and military leaders in the United States, Canada, Britain, France and Germany. This caused some confusion in the leadership of each country. Only Britain saw this as a possible prelude to war. They quietly warned the NATO countries of the danger and suggested that all those countries go on heightened military alert. Only France and Germany listened. The U.S. and Canada feared that this would be an overreaction which would aggravate the situation. The nations of the Alliance were, of course, proclaiming innocence, feigning offense that the West would even think of accusing them of such a thing. China reiterated that it only was taking that which rightfully belonged to China.

Then Christmas Eve arrived. In the Mountain West, we all went inside our homes and closed our doors. Anna and I gathered our family around us and prayed for the Lord's protection through what we knew was coming. We had planned carefully and had our food storage inside where we could access it. We also had many five-gallon buckets of water set aside. In addition, we had prepared a portable toilet for sanitation, and we had some fuel for cooking. This was fuel that could be burned safely indoors. Then we waited.

We had a crank-operated radio and with that we could get some news from the outside, but it was spotty at best for several weeks. We knew that being in close quarters for an extended time would create tension, so we had activities for everyone. To keep us occupied and sane, a strict schedule was established for the daytime. There were school classes for the younger children. They were taught by the older children. Clean-up duties were also assigned. We held scripture study in the evenings, and there were times for games and fun. We did store games. That turned out to be one of the best things we did. And of course, there were meals. Preparing them and cleaning up afterward took a lot of time, but was a welcome part of each day. We even had some sweets stored to add to the diet. Variety was important. In this manner, we passed the time for those two weeks. Outside, it was a different story.

Around the country, December 25th began with people getting up, opening presents and generally having a good time. By early afternoon, when folks were going out to visit family and friends, or sitting down to their Christmas feast, disaster struck. The first wave of missiles came in at about 1:00 p.m. Mountain time. They hit cities like New York, Boston, Seattle, LA, San Diego, Washington, D.C., Atlanta, Chicago, Kansas City, New Orleans, and many more. The list was huge. As we sat glued to our radios, reports trickled in - a city here, a military base there. They hit each strategic base they could, except for those they already occupied. They hit bases in Southern California, Utah, Kansas, other Midwestern areas, and the East Coast. Hill Air force Base and Nellis Air Force Base were among those hit. That meant we would be downwind of any fallout. The reports indicated that the bombs were nuclear, and were of the type that were designed to kill people without destroying all the buildings. Do not get me wrong. A huge chunk of each area hit was leveled, and fires were started that spread terribly. In that first hour alone, the death toll was in the tens of millions and the devastation was enormous.

The defense system of the United States did pick up the incoming missiles, and many missiles were fired in response. The problem was that some missile sites delayed, and so never got to fire. They could not believe that this was actually happening, and were, as a consequence, destroyed. Most U.S. missiles that were deployed found their targets. We learned later that much damage was done to military and city sites throughout Russia and China. However, those countries knew that there would be a retaliation, and had moved all important equipment and people out of harm's way. This made our counterstrike much less effective. After all, they had the advantage of foreknowledge, and so could prepare.

A second wave of missiles came in about 3:00 p.m. Mountain time. These added a new dimension to the war. The missiles were loaded with biological warheads. They exploded to release huge amounts of horrible diseases onto the people of America. They were combination type organisms that we later learned had been genetically engineered, with qualities from organisms such as anthrax, small pox, E Bola and more. Each warhead contained not one organism, but several. This was a shotgun approach; if one organism did not work, another one would. These bombs usually exploded high in the air, spreading their deadly contents over many miles. These missiles were not only fired at all our major cities, but were designed to explode at an altitude where the prevailing winds would spread their venom over several states at a time. Some of these organisms had the affect of eating the flesh off of the body in the most gruesome manner. These diseases spread as an overflowing plague that caused the most terrible suffering possible. The reports coming in on our radio were so horrible at times that we would turn it off, just to have a break from the awful news. Over a period of about a week, more than 100 million people died from the combined effects of the two initial missile attacks alone.

Around the country, those who lived through the Christmas Day attack went inside to hide. But many did not have enough food or water stored in their homes, and so when hunger and thirst became pressing enough, they would venture outside only to find themselves dying from the plagues or radiation. Those who had food and water stored, stayed inside for the most part. Warnings were issued all over the country from those radio and TV stations that still operated. The warnings told people to stay inside as much as possible until the radiation and diseases subsided. Power was lost in most areas since people could no longer get to the generating plants or maintain delivery systems. For the same reason, water and sewer systems soon stopped functioning as well. As for radio and TV, some continued operation because of emergency preparations that had been made years before for military reasons. These few radio and TV stations became the voice that told what was going on around the country.

In Washington, D.C., the entire government structure was in shambles. The main political leaders were all dead. However, many of the military leaders had managed to survive because they had heeded the warning from the British, though our military in general was in bad shape. The military had tried to move what hardware it could to safety, but had still lost much. Their ability to fight had been severely crippled by their defeat in their war against the West. Now the missile attacks had made that even worse. They did manage to pull what military they could back away from the most vulnerable areas, and they sequestered them from the suspected attack.

People were warned to stay inside until the radiation could decay down to a less dangerous level, and the disease organisms could die off. Unfortunately, this proved to be an almost impossible request, because people were rapidly running out of anything to eat. Manufacturing stopped almost completely and, therefore, no one was producing food. The road system, and all that related to it, was nonfunctioning. Many oil refining areas had been hit and so no gasoline or fuel was produced. Transportation was by foot. Only the military had any fuel, and that was in storage tanks. When it was gone they were through.

The U.S. military established a new defense center in Illinois. The main leaders of each branch went there. The Army, Marines, Air Force and Navy set up a coordinated command structure. They knew they were in trouble, but had to respond in some manner. They could do little for several weeks until the radiation decayed down and the diseases were less of a threat.

Out West, in the area controlled by the government of Christ, we watched and waited. Missiles had hit here too, but we were more prepared, hence, we were much less affected. Most of our people had already been moved out of the large cities, and so were not in the target areas of the attack. All military hardware had already been taken to safe areas, and so was not destroyed when the western bases were bombed. We had not been as badly damaged because of our preparations. This gave us a distinct advantage.

As for the Alliance, after the initial missile attacks, they did nothing for several weeks. They, too, were waiting until it was safe before they would send their people out for the invasion. The United States military leaders were puzzled by this silence, and wondered what was next. They did not have to wait long.

Across the country, the situation was one of horror, misery and suffering. About the second week of January, the seaports and airports that the Alliance forces had seized were opened for a flood of foreign military hardware to come into the continental U.S. Armadas of ships docked with all manner of tanks, personnel carriers, support equipment, soldiers of every stripe, and supplies. Planes landed in squadron after squadron of activity. The Alliance knew exactly what it was doing. It had carefully avoided bombing those areas it controlled, and their troops had immediately seized control of each spot when the missile attack began. Now, it was all too easy to pour their militaries onto American soil. No Utah or Omaha Beach was necessary.

The treachery of our past leaders had left our country wide open for this invasion; now it was here. Some of our own leaders had sold their influence for money from foreign countries. Now those countries were calling in their favors. We were paying a terrible price for not punishing those traitorous leaders when we had a chance. This could have been avoided if only we had had the courage to do the right thing back then. But we did not. We did the politically expedient thing. Now we were getting our due.

By the end of January, the Alliance had solid control of the seaports and airports it had occupied, including the territory for miles around each one. There were almost 100,000 Russian troops on the east coast from Florida to New York. A similar number of Chinese troops were now on the west coast between San Diego and Seattle, with the largest concentration in the Southern California area. There were about 30,000 Islamic troops on the gulf coast in the area of Mississippi and Alabama.

Invasion

At this point, the United States military felt like attack was advisable before these troops left their base ports of operation. It was the beginning of February. A series of air operations began against the biggest concentrations of foreign troops along the east, west and gulf coasts. These military campaigns were intensely fought on both sides as jets sparred in the skies, bombs were dropped, and missiles were fired. The troops of the Alliance fought effectively and turned back the U.S. forces. Then the Alliance began a counter-series of air strikes against the U.S. military positions. The effect was devastating. The American military was too weakened. It could not expel the invaders, and indeed, could not stop their counterattacks, or the destruction that they inflicted. This whole process only took several weeks.

Now the Alliance forces moved out. It was Valentine's Day. Their numbers were growing daily as more troops came in on all coasts. Remember, they did not want to conquer the population; they wanted to annihilate it. They planned to empty the land as they moved inward from the oceans. Each day brought new reports of massacre and genocide. There was nowhere to go to for justice. With the missile attack on December 25th, the United Nations had collapsed. The World Court was essentially defunct since Europe was undergoing its own attack and occupation. Things in Europe were desperate. In America, the foreign troops moved systematically outward from their bases through all the towns and cities. None was missed. Each town and city was methodically searched, house by house, building by building. Even isolated farmhouses were searched. Anyone found was killed. Sometimes they tortured or raped people before killing them. Fear spread everywhere as the local citizens fled before the advancing Alliance troops.

The United States military repeatedly established defensive lines in an attempt to stop the advancing Alliance. They chose strategic areas along the Appalachian Mountains, the hill country of the Southern states and the hills and mountains of California, Oregon and Washington State. They prepared defensive positions in each of these areas. They called for all citizens to help in the fight. All able-bodied men joined or were forced to

155

join. Even the women had to fight. Now they were wishing everyone still had the guns they had confiscated many months back, but it was too late for that.

The remaining population of the coastal states ran to the U.S. military for protection. Those who were strong among them were inducted into the military, and the rest were left to fend for themselves. Anyone not of use to the military was left to die of exposure and starvation. Old people, the weak and children by the tens of thousands were abandoned everywhere. Then, when the advancing Alliance reached them, it killed them. No mercy was shown, not even for babies. Starvation and famine were more common than not.

As the Alliance reached each one of the defensive U.S. positions, a terrible battle ensued that often lasted for days or weeks, with millions dying along the way. Ultimately, the Alliance would win and the U.S. forces would pull back to a new defensive position to wait for the Alliance to reach it. The Alliance would then move forward toward the next defensive position, methodically searching each dwelling, town and city, killing all it found. When it would reach the next U.S. defensive position, another terrible fight would ensue until the United States military was forced to retreat again, and so it went. Each time the U.S. troops pulled back, they took all the able-bodied population they could find with them, forcing them to fight. Anyone not useful to them was refused help, and left for the Alliance to kill.

Behind the ever-advancing front formed by the Alliance, there was a landscape of desolation and death. No one buried the dead; they lay about in heaps, thrown there by their conquerors. Their bodies rotted in the sun and were fed upon by the wild animals that now seemed to be the only inhabitants of these empty cities. Even the birds of the air ate the dead bodies. The stench was so bad as to almost cause death just to breathe it.

In this manner the Russian, Chinese and Islamic troops advanced. They moved fitfully inland as they conquered each defensive position. The process took many months. Between the Alliance troops killing everyone in their path of advance, and the U.S. troops pulling in everyone in their path of retreat, the land of America was being emptied. By May, the Russians and Islams had reached inland in a front that arched from Dallas, Texas through western Tennessee, over and up through central Kentucky, and north into Ohio and Lake Eerie. Even the eastern end of Canada was invaded. In the West, the Chinese had moved their front inland in a pattern that extended from San Diego inland to the Imperial Valley, and then north along the Sierra Nevada Mountains up past the Cascade Mountains, and down to the Seattle area.

Back in January, the leaders of the government of Christ contacted the United States military leaders, and informed them that if they would join us, accept the Constitution in its original form, repent, abide by our laws, and accept Christ as their king, we could be united again. Then we would help them defeat the Alliance. We offered amnesty to all. The U.S. military refused this offer outright. They said that they did not need our help and would never submit to Christ or His kingdom. In early May, we reiterated the offer, but again, they refused.

It is interesting to note that when people reach a certain point of wickedness, they become so drunken with evil that they would rather die than repent. This was the spiritual state of most people who were still alive outside of the Mountain West. We were deeply saddened to see such hate and evil in a people who once were good. Truly, Satan had them in his chains and was dragging them down to hell.

Throughout the West we waited. After the two-week period of isolation in our homes, we began, on a limited basis, to move about again, doing our work. By the end of February the biological threat was gone and we could move freely outdoors. The refusal of the United States military to accept Christ as their king left us as spectators on the sidelines of a ghastly drama that unfolded beyond our mountain bulwarks. Our political and religious leaders met and sought counsel from the Lord. They were instructed to have our people prepare themselves spiritually and physically to build Zion. We were to attend the temples as often as possible to strengthen ourselves, and we were to prepare temporally as well. We were instructed to ready our homes, our businesses and our farms. There was much to do, and this preparation was important. We were told that our military would be called up one more time, and that following this, we would not be threatened again by any outside power. The importance of spiritual preparation was emphasized again, because before we could build a Zion city, we must first be a Zion people.

At the beginning of April, our defense force was called up again. Robert, his friends and I had to leave our home and go back to our original units. The generals and the chief commander were already prepared for what lay ahead. A great deal of careful reconnaissance had been taking place for months. They had been studying the movements of the Alliance troops as they advanced from both the east and the west coasts. Our troops were moved into their original positions along our mountain borders, where we waited. Our equipment and ammunition were readied, and we practiced and prepared. We were instructed to wait upon the Lord. We were told that things would be brought to a head soon, and that we needed to be prepared physically and, above all, spiritually. The process of calling all our people back was accomplished within just a few weeks.

The United States military was now tiring. They had been fighting a losing battle for many months, and with each day they lost more ground. By this time, the people of the country had been gathered into the United States forces. Even the states geographically removed from the fighting had sent most of their remaining able-bodied men, and even women, to the fronts. Most of the population of the country was not concentrated along these defensive fronts. Except for the West, most of the states were virtually empty of their former inhabitants. The situation was worse than desperate. It was rapidly becoming apparent that this would be their last stand. The Alliance sensed this and accelerated their advance. Their attacks grew even more ferocious and vicious.

In the second week of May, a major Alliance thrust occurred on both the east and west fronts. Massive bombing and missile attacks began that lasted for days. The pounding was horrendous; the losses to the U.S. troops were devastating. Specifically, the command centers for the US military were hit hardest. Many U.S. leaders were killed, and what little order was left began to break down. After a week of this terrible bombing, the Alliance troops pushed forward with such force that they smashed through the U.S. lines, which crumbled and fell back. The U.S. forces were in such disarray, that they broke and ran. The quickest among them were able to escape. Those who were not as fast were caught by the surging Alliance army. All those who were captured were killed on the spot, or they were tortured, abused and then killed. Many of these invaders committed the vilest types of atrocities. They rapidly advanced and perceived themselves as superior. They boasted of their greatness, and bragged of how they were the conquerors of America.

Their leaders were so certain of victory, that they spoke openly of how they would crush the resistance in the central and western parts of the continent. Then they would divide the spoils. They could almost taste their victory. They ridiculed America for its' past arrogance. They repeatedly mocked the Christian background of the United States and Canada, asking, "Where is your God now if He is so great?" They did not understand that the people they had conquered were not true followers of Christ. The true followers of Christ had been driven out to the West more than six months before. Indeed, the reason for the Alliance's success was precisely because the U.S. troops and citizens were no longer followers of Christ and His teachings at all. The leaders of the Alliance continued to boast that their might and technology had defeated America.

The Alliance raced forward. In the east, they pushed their control inland in an arc that now extended from the Texas panhandle north to Kansas City and then up the Missouri River into central Canada. What was left of the United States troops had fallen back to that point and then somehow managed to regroup. In the West, the Alliance had pushed inland until their line of advance extended up the Colorado River to Las

Vegas, and then went north, roughly following the California-Nevada line, up the Sierra Nevada Mountains into western Oregon and Washington, and even into coastal British Columbia.

To the outside world, it seemed that all was lost for the United States of America and Canada. The situation was little better in Europe. The combined forces of the communist and Islamic dictators were on the verge of achieving their goal.

At the beginning of June, the U.S. forces were almost worn out. The ferocious battles in May had cost them dearly. Most of their leaders and at least half of their troops had been lost as well. This did not even count the many civilian casualties, which by now were so huge that people had stopped counting them months ago. The total loss of life in the United States was more than 200 million people. The magnitude of events over the last year and a half was so great that they did not seem real. The continual barrage of reports with extreme numbers and words had numbed us all to the reality of what was transpiring. A few years ago, the thought that most of the population of the country would be dead two years hence was unimaginable, as was the idea of our homeland being invaded. Anyone suggesting such would have been labeled as an extremist. Now, both these dire thoughts were a suffocating nightmare that seemed to go on and on without relief. Only in the West was there any peace.

The ragtag crew of U.S. troops now put up a fight that can only be understood in the context of the desperate struggle of a people fighting against extinction. Their numbers, now diminished to a tiny fraction of America's once vast population, showed that they were at the point of do or die. If they failed now, all was lost. Now, a change occurred at this time. The more wicked part of the population was dead. Those people who were still alive, were made up of that part of the population which still had some goodness left hidden within it. They now humbled themselves and admitted that they had been wrong to reject the righteous. They lamented the sins of their past. They sorrowed for their willingness to sacrifice truth to the demands of expediency, greed and lust. As the battle became a desperate fight for survival, they petitioned the kingdom of Christ to save them. They admitted that they had been wrong; they swore to serve Him and obey His law and the Constitution in its original form, if only the defenders of the West would help them defeat the Alliance.

Our western leaders immediately accepted their petition. They had been waiting for this. It was early June and our troops were ordered to immediately move out of the mountain bases where we were waiting. We were instructed to move forward to within one hundred miles of each front. My unit set up camp in central Kansas. The Lord told us that if we were righteous, He would fight our battles as he did against Egypt and Assyria of old. He said He would strengthen our arms, as David of old, and that He would drive this army from our land, back to where they came from. We were taught that this would be done with great power so that all the world would know that it was Christ who had saved us. The power of His holy arm would be so evident that we would not be able to take credit to ourselves for our deliverance.

We were again instructed that there should be no wanton killing. As long as the enemy was retreating, we were to let them leave. We were also informed that tens of thousands of these soldiers from Russia, China and the Islamic countries would surrender and beg to stay. Christ told us that they would be from among those who had not participated in the worst atrocities. These would be the people whose hearts were not past feeling, and who would see in the kingdom of Christ something they desired. We were instructed to disarm all who surrendered. We were to put them into camps where they could be taught the truth. We were told that eventually they would become one with us and would later serve to teach their countrymen the Gospel.

With these instructions, we arrived at our one hundred-mile perimeter where we camped. The chief commander of our troops called for a truce, in order that he might speak to the leader of the armies of the Alliance. The truce was granted at the beginning of the second week of June. By this time all the remaining U.S. troops had been placed under our military leader's command. We promised the Alliance that the original U.S. military troops would be pulled back from the front as a show of good faith. The Alliance accepted this, assuming that this would ensure that much more land for them with less resistance after the truce.

The Alliance was aware that the defense forces of the West had pulled out of the mountains, and had advanced to within one hundred miles of the front. They calculated that this would not pose any real threat to them since they had essentially already defeated the superior force of the United States military. What they expected was that we would want to surrender. They actually thought our leaders would offer to sign articles of surrender, accepting our defeat. They planned to refuse, because their unaltered goal still was to kill everyone and free-up the land and wealth for themselves. Boy were they surprised!

By this time, the original U.S. troops had been withdrawn back from the front. They joined us at our positions. Each U.S. military unit was placed under one of our captains and they were quickly integrated into our forces. We explained our orders to them. Then, the meeting between the leaders of the Alliance and our leaders took place in a no-man's land near Kansas City. Our chief commander gave them an ultimatum from the kingdom of Christ, that all Alliance troops were to be withdrawn from our soil, or they would be destroyed by the power of Christ. The generals of the Alliance were at first amazed, and then incensed! Instead of the expected offer of surrender, their enemy, whom they perceived as weak and defeated, had just told them to leave or be destroyed! The generals of the Alliance left the meeting in anger, threatening to crush us.

Our chief commander returned and put us on alert. We were instructed to operate as we had done in our first war with the U.S. Army. We were to use our antiaircraft missiles to shoot down their planes, and we were to use our Priesthood power to send their missiles back. We were told that many planes would fly very high overhead going to the Salt Lake City area. We were to let them pass. These planes would drop thousands of paratroopers along the Wasatch Front. We were told not to worry. The Lord would deal with them. The Alliance thought it would strike at the heart of the western defense force, which it mistakenly thought was in Salt Lake City. We were also strictly forbidden to advance at this time. We were only to defend. We were not to advance until the Lord had broken the backbone of the Alliance.

On June 12th, the Alliance struck. Waves of planes bombed our positions. We were prepared with antiaircraft missiles and caused tremendous damage. They were not expecting this response since they had not encountered any of these missiles for two months. They were even more astonished when the missiles they launched returned and exploded. They had no explanation for such behavior by their missiles, which did great damage to their own positions. They felt much better about their paratrooper campaign, as thousands of their soldiers rained down from the sky over the Salt Lake City area. To their amazement, these advance units began sending back reports of a city deserted. The battle was not going according to plan.

On June 13th, the Lord struck back. It was still dark when the first meteors streaked overhead, trailing fire as they went. At first, there were only a few. We looked up, as I remembered doing on scout campouts, marveling at nature's fireworks in the sky. Then the numbers increased. By sunrise there were thousands of meteors tracing their way overhead. Invariably, they all headed for the Alliance front lines. This continued for hours, hail mingled with fire, raining down from the sky upon our enemies! Our communications soon revealed that this unearthly phenomenon was occurring all up and down the eastern and western fronts. This torrential rain of fire was crushing the Alliance forces, while we remained untouched and unharmed! I was amazed at the Lord's accuracy in employing such a destructive force.

On a small scale, I had witnessed such a thing once long ago on a campout in the Uintah Mountains, but never had I expected to witness it on such a grand scale as this. By late afternoon, we received reports of similar destruction all over the globe. Cities were being leveled, and giant fires raged. We heard calls for help, as massive firestorms swept over entire regions in diverse countries, reducing vast areas to ashes. Worst of all, were the distressed cries of alarm as nation after nation reported that the hail was destroying their crops. The specter of a worldwide famine loomed like some fictional monster on the horizon. By nightfall, the rain of terror ceased; the devastation left behind was beyond words. It turned out that this was only a prelude to what occurred next.

That night and the next morning were spent taking inventory of our situation. As it turned out, the western areas had been largely spared, with the exception of the Salt Lake City area, where the paratroopers were. There was a feeling of relief and gratitude as we realized what the Lord had done for us. We were to find out that He was not done.

On the afternoon of June 14, a massive earthquake shook the ground where I was. It hit about 3:30 p.m.. The force was so great that the very earth opened up in places in large cracks. These cracks would open and close, swallowing whatever fell in. The main quake lasted for almost 30 minutes, its intensity waxing and waning. It was impossible to stand up during much of that time, and most buildings collapsed. We learned later that the cause of the quake was an asteroid hitting the Pacific Ocean. The asteroid was approximately one-and-a-half miles in diameter. The force of its impact had caused the tectonic plates of the earth to jiggle and shift all over the globe. The result was a series of worldwide earthquakes that caused considerable changes in the earth's geography. There were reports of coastal areas and islands sinking into the sea, and of new islands being pushed up. There was also a large tidal wave that radiated outward from the crash site of the asteroid. It inundated the coastal regions of the entire Pacific rim. The waves were so huge in some areas that they went many miles inland, before they flowed back out into the ocean. Entire cities were washed away. On top of that, a dark cloud of pulverized debris spread outward over the planet, darkening the sun for several days. Following this, the sky had an odd gray color to it for weeks. This did not turn out to be the destructive, months long darkness that scientists had predicted for such an event, but it was impressive, nevertheless.

The Alliance forces had been decimated. The initial meteor shower had destroyed more than half of their machinery. It killed thirty percent of their men, and left almost that many more with injuries, great and small. The earthquake furthered the destruction, as the cracks swallowed up their men and equipment whole. In their home countries, the devastation was bad, which depressed their morale. They were informed that supplies would be harder to come by. In China, the coastal flooding from the asteroid killed almost one hundred million people. The world began to see that man's power is nothing compared to God's power.

The main leader of the Alliance called an emergency meeting. The damage that they had sustained, along with the feeling of many of their people that God was protecting the people of Christ (or Zion as they were becoming known), was causing their resolve to waver. It took all of that leader's persuasive skills to keep the Alliance from withdrawing. Their leader told them that this was just a chance thing, a one-in-a-million year event. He said that they were so close to victory that they could not turn back now. They had only to attack and finish off Zion, and then they could divide the spoils. He reminded them of their great victories in North America up until this time, and pointed out that they still had a significant weapons advantage. He urged that they press forward and finish the job.

Then he asked, "What are the chances of another asteroid hitting the earth? They just got lucky this time. It was not their God protecting them. We will be fine from now on."

Was he ever in for a surprise. However, the Alliance bought his arguments, and rallied around him. Word was sent to their troops in America to attack and finish the job.

Our leaders knew this first series of destructions would not be adequate to convince our enemies to withdraw. They sent a second warning to the generals and political leaders of the Alliance. They warned them that if the Alliance did not withdraw and return home, that the Lord would send down worse destructions upon them. Like Pharaoh of old, these leaders rejected the words of inspired men, and they regrouped. They prepared to strike again.

This whole process of meetings, regrouping, and preparation to attack, took about three weeks. During this time, little happened along the eastern or western fronts. Basically, we waited. We were told to be prepared for another attack, but we were still only to defend ourselves. The instructions were the same as before, shoot down their planes, use the Priesthood to send back their missiles, and let the paratroopers land in Salt Lake City. The Alliance decided to send more paratroopers in to take the metropolitan area of Salt Lake City. The first group of paratroopers had been nearly destroyed by the meteors and earthquakes. The few who were left were isolated and unable to carry out their mission. More were to be sent.

On July 10th, the Alliance attacked again. They sent their planes and missiles. We shot them down and sent the missiles back, with the same results as before. The paratroopers descended upon Salt Lake City again and began to fan out, but they found themselves occupying an empty city, filled with damaged or destroyed buildings, and little more. Little of any consequence was accomplished. After three days of this futile effort of bombardment and occupation, the Alliance decided to initiate a coordinated ground attack.

On July 13th, the Lord struck again. It was mid-afternoon again, just like the month before, when the earth heaved beneath our feet. Just prior to this, we were notified that the Alliance army had started moving, and would reach our lines by 5:00 p.m. that day. It was never to be. As the earth shook violently, the very forces of nature seemed to rage in anger. This was the fourth earthquake in less than two years, and of the four, this was by far the worst. The very planet rocked in its orbit. As I looked up, the sun moved erratically across the sky. The ground again cracked open and slammed shut. It was impossible to stand. Lava began to spew forth from some of the cracks. Flowing rivers of molten lava alternated with explosions of fiery rock. These rocks rained down upon the Alliance forces. Once again the devastation was directed toward our enemies. Even the lava seemed to find their camps.

As for us, we were little affected by all of this, except for the quaking of the earth, which did not hurt us other than to give us a good scare. For the thrill seekers among us, it was a real "E" ticket ride. The quaking lasted for five hours, alternating between times of big and little motion, with brief interludes of stability in-between. At this same time, huge storms rolled in, and the heavens turned black with menacing clouds. Then the lightening and thunder began like I had never seen before. Torrential rains and tornadoes followed. Large clumpings of tornadoes moved through the Alliance camps, carrying away men and machinery alike. Tanks, planes, trucks and buildings all were swept away. Between the earthquakes, the volcanoes, and the storms, the enemy camps, both east and west, were laid waste. The damage was so complete that their equipment was destroyed or gone, and most of their men and leaders were dead.

Reports came in about the Wasatch Front. There the quake had opened the earth in large chasms, and volcanoes had erupted. Even some of the mighty mountains to the east of the city had sunk away. New ones had risen up in other areas where there had been no mountains. Storms had raged with horrible lightening and thunder; and there was something else that happened that was so unusual. Huge fountains of water shot skyward from the depths of the Great Salt Lake. It was described as if it were a series of giant, unending geysers that ran for miles. The water level on the lake began to rise rapidly. Within only a few hours, the water was lapping at the lower windows of the Salt Lake Temple. As for the paratroopers, this process of volcanoes, earthquakes, floods and storms had wiped them out. Only a few survived, and they surrendered themselves to our troops.

The flood level of the Great Salt Lake lasted only a few weeks. Delayed fissures in the mountains far to the north opened a drainage that dropped the lake back almost to its former level. We soon learned that, due to elevation changes, the drainage was permanent, and the Great Salt Lake soon became a fresh-water lake teeming with fish, and it had wildlife all around its shores. Between the volcanoes and flooding, the lands along the Wasatch Front had been cleansed and enriched. It became very productive, much more than before.

Back at our camp in Kansas, it was several days before we received reports from outside of America. Then the news began streaming in. The last quake had been caused by a comet hitting the earth. It was larger in size than the asteroid. It had struck in eastern Russia, in Siberia. The impact had jolted the very earth in its orbit, causing it to wobble erratically on its axis. This caused the earth to sit more upright on its axis. That in turn caused a moderation in the earth's climate and major changes in its weather patterns. The impact of the comet had blown another cloud of debris into the atmosphere that again darkened the sun for several days. The comet contained within itself a chemical of some type that rained down over Russia and China. This chemical temporarily poisoned most of the fresh water, and led to the deaths of hundreds of millions of people in those countries.

Other news reports spoke of entire cities collapsed in ruins. In some places, the volcanoes continued spewing their ash into the air for months. Tidal waves, tornadoes, and famine were events that played no favorites in their distribution. Every country seemed to have some of each.

Beyond the natural upheaval, political upheaval broke out everywhere. People in countries all over the world were tired of being lied to and abused. Many began to see these devastations for what they really were, the punishing hand of God to a wicked world; they blamed their leaders for creating the evil that had brought this down on their heads. Civil wars now sprang up like dandelions, appearing overnight throughout the nations of the earth. In addition, the people of the world had been watching with interest the turn of events in America. The change in fortunes for the Alliance in the last month and a half was obvious to all, and they caught the message. The people of Zion, in the western United States, were truly powerful and terrible. God was with them. Who could possibly stand against them?

The fractured and crushed Alliance armies pulled what men they could back together. Our chief commander now ordered us to move forward. We were told to attack the Alliance positions, our goal being to destroy their large weapons of war. We targeted these few weapons. If they attempted to use a tank, truck or plane, we destroyed it. As we advanced, the demoralized armies of our enemies fell back. Any thought of attack was gone from the Alliance. There was a general feeling among them that God was helping us, and that they could not stand against us. Our slow, methodical advance started them into a retreat. At first it was slow, but then it turned into a fearful run for the coasts. This was the case for most of their troops, but not all. Some units literally surrendered en masse. They dropped their weapons and came to us with hands up. They said they knew God was with us and they wished to stay. This happened among the Russians and the Chinese, and to a lesser extent, among the Islams. We found ourselves with tens of thousands of foreign troops assigned to camps in areas as diverse as Texas, Illinois, Missouri, Alabama, California and Oregon, to mention only a few. These camps were quickly organized into working towns with everyone contributing to help provide for food, shelter and clothing.

We had the added advantage of having among us people who had served missions in the native countries of these people. They spoke the languages and understood the cultures of each group. Best of all, they had a deep love for these people. The returned missionaries now began to teach these people about the restored Church of Jesus Christ, with its priesthood and ordinances of salvation and exaltation. They taught them of the kingdom of Christ and how His political government worked. The missionaries taught them of faith, repentance, baptism and the gift of the Holy Ghost. They also told them that they could be forgiven of their sins. We were amazed that most of these men came into the Church over the next many months, and were baptized. In time, many would return to their homelands as missionaries.

As the Alliance retreated, we received word that an army was approaching from the north, from the Arctic regions. It had already reached northern Saskatchewan, Manitoba and Ontario. Some of the Alliance forces that were retreating north of the Great Lakes encountered advance parties from this army.

Apparently, a few skirmishes occurred, but the Alliance was no match for this northern army. Our leaders were told by the Prophet not to interfere or impede this army's progress. This was the vanguard of the returning ten tribes. We were to welcome them and aid them, and we sent emissaries to greet them. Christ had already revealed to the Prophet that this group would come on the heels of the retreating invaders. We were not surprised to find that a plan was already in place to meet the needs of these ten tribes of Israel. After all, we had before us an empty continent to fill and cities waiting to be rebuilt.

At this same time, we were informed that large camps of Lamanites were coming up from the south. Some had already traveled from South America and were growing in number as they moved northward through Central America and Mexico. Their advance party was already in southern Texas. Again, we were instructed not to interfere or impede their progress. These descendants of Joseph were coming under the inspiration of the Lord to help us build the New Jerusalem. The ten tribes were to assist in this great work as well. We also sent emissaries to greet the Lamanites; and plans were already in place for their needs to be met.

Our military completed the expulsion of the invaders from our land, both east and west. People are beginning to return to their homes, businesses and farms along the Wasatch Front. They are finding that the soil is many times more fertile than it was before the calamities.

Now, it is early October, almost two years since the financial collapse occurred, and the last of the invaders are gone or have surrendered and joined us. The country is again united; the war is over; there is peace. Not the enforced peace that the nations once used, but true peace that comes from personal righteousness, justice and a righteous self government. This justice is no longer the counterfeit fare we were fed by the politically correct deceivers of a few years ago. It is the true justice of Jesus Christ that is based on divine truth. It reminds us that we are responsible for our own actions. It has restored to us true freedom of religion, allowing an unfettered search for truth. Evil no longer flourishes in the name of tolerance. Contention and divisiveness are no longer accepted in the name of diversity. Immorality and the killing of the unborn are no longer allowed in the false name of choice. Dishonesty, deception and greed are no longer accepted in the name of being a shrewd businessman or politician. Last but not least, big government is no longer allowed in the name of helping to save us from ourselves.

The oppressive weight of evil that once permeated our country and government is gone. Divine law is our standard of life at all levels. People are breathing free, and are opening up in an easy friendship that was rare in the recent past. It is good to be free again! It is good to be free!

CHAPTER 11

RESTITUTION

Change is now the order of the day and its magnitude is crystal clear in retrospect. The changes that have transpired are remarkable, even dazzling, and cover all fronts. It is difficult to believe that so much dramatic change could occur in such a short period of time. The America I see now is nothing like the one I was so much a part of only two years ago. I guess that is why I have written this book, to record forever after what has happened to America and how it has affected my family and me. We are still assessing the damage from the war, but that will be done soon. As I view America, I am filled with sadness for the past, and hope and anticipation for the future. Soon, the rebuilding will begin in earnest as we prepare for the New Jerusalem and a Zion society that is even now expanding to fill the continent.

My military unit, along with most of the others, was released to go home. It is good to be with my wife and family again. Even Robert is back, but I do not think he will stay for long. There are so many opportunities available for him. Deanna and Kayla will be with Anna and me a little while yet, and so our home should have some youthful excitement for a few more years. They are back in school and I am back at work trying to get my business going again.

The physical changes caused in the geography of the earth by the fourth earthquake have changed our climate a lot. Isaiah said that streams would appear on the hills and mountains in the day the towers fell; that is happening. The amount of rain we receive has increased dramatically. Where the West used to be arid, now the average rainfall could be as much as fifty inches a year if this continues like this. All this gentle rain has caused streams and rivers to appear where once only dust blew in the hot wind. This winter is not yet cold, and it looks like maybe our winters will be permanently milder. The meteorologists are already predicting that the summers will not be as hot either. The dry lake beds are now filled with water, and the western United States presents an abundant scene of lakes, streams and rivers everywhere. The elevation changes in the West have ended the Great Basin, as it now drains easily both north and south. The nice thing about these rains is that they are gentle and are interspersed with plenty of sunny days. The West has become a land of many waters again, as some of the old Indian legends claim it once was.

As the diverse parts of the House of Israel come together to live in America as one people, there is a practical problem. Each group speaks a different language. Consequently, Christ has given us a new language to speak. I guess I should not call it new, because it is the original language of Adam. It is just new to us. Christ has told us that it is a perfect language. He has promised us that if we will all learn it, it will dramatically improve our ability to express ourselves and to communicate one with another; there will be less misunderstanding. There is also a new writing system with the Adamic language. It is somewhat overwhelming, but Christ also promised that as we endeavor to learn this new language, with it's writing system, the gift of the Holy Ghost will help us. I saw this work on my mission as I learned the Indonesian language. I know that if the Holy Spirit can help tens of thousands of missionaries learn other tongues, it can help us learn this one. Soon my English will be a thing of the past, as will the individual languages of the other groups of the House of Israel. I expect that by this time next year, all interactions will be conducted in the Adamic tongue.

We have been told that next spring construction on the New Jerusalem will begin. The Prophet, along with other leaders and workers, has traveled to what was once Independence, Missouri. We understand that they are laying out the center place of the city, with the anticipated temple complex, businesses,

174

schools, farms and homes. There is so much work to be done, but there will be many hands to participate. They are also designing city plots that will be spaced outward around the central one. Each additional city plot will be separated one from another by miles of farmland and forest. This will prevent the creation of an inhuman megalopolis like the ones that once developed in America. I find the idea fascinating, and can hardly wait to see the result.

We are also informed that the meeting with Adam at Adam-Ondi-Ahman has already occurred. Apparently this event occurred before the crisis had even attained its 'full height.' The Lord's Prophets from each dispensation were there, along with many saints, dating back to the days of Adam. The meeting was apparently very large. Christ was in attendance, as well. He is now exercising His right to reign over the earth. Official notices have again been given to all nations that they must submit to His righteous rule. I understand that a mixed response is coming in from the nations of the earth. It will be interesting to watch how all this unfolds. One thing for sure, all the nations of the earth have great respect, sometimes bordering on fear, for Zion. After what happened to the Alliance, no one dares attack us, and many nations have sent ambassadors. They are seeking to join us and have said they will accept the law of Christ. They have asked for emissaries from Zion to be sent to teach them our laws. They have also asked us to teach them how to administer those laws in righteousness. However, not all nations are responding so favorably. Some are just standing back in fear, not quite knowing what to do.

As I look back, I can see that Isaiah's many prophesies that the world would attack both Zion and Jerusalem have been and are still being fulfilled. Everyone knew about the battle of Armageddon that was to come. Few, however, understood Isaiah's words about the attack that was to come against the people of Christ in America. Now, hindsight makes that so clear. As for Armageddon, it is another story for another time.

Isaiah had another insight which now is a stark reality. The calamities and wars of the last few years left a great many more women alive than men. The ratio actually is about seven women to one man. It is impressive that Isaiah has consistently, repeatedly and accurately prophesied the future. His prophesy of how this time of trouble was to be resolved has now been fulfilled, as has his prophesy of the way the Lord was going to resolve the situation of seven women to one man. Step by step, we are seeing all things restored, both physically and spiritually. The House of Israel is being gathered; the land is being healed and the Lord's law is returning in all its fullness and glory. This latter restoration is occurring through the Lord's appointed pattern of His Prophet and apostles. In the past, many apostates sought to take this authority upon themselves, but in this they were gravely mistaken. The Lord's house is a house of order, and He is able to do his own work in the way He has established. Much that is wonderful and marvelous is now pouring forth through his prophets and apostles.

The Lord is directing that one last time before His second coming, the missionaries of the Church are to be sent out to the nations of the earth, especially the heathen nations. Not only are the young men of the Church being called, but those from years past who served in these countries of the world are now being called to go out again. Through the years, many men in the Church have learned diverse languages. These same men have now been through the refining process of the cleansing hand of the Lord. They have years of experience in Priesthood leadership, and have the testimony of Christ firmly planted within their hearts. Now, they are responding by the tens of thousands to the Lord's call to serve again. I am guessing that by the time this process is finally completed, their number will reach one hundred forty-four thousand, and will be another fulfillment of prophesy.

As for the rest of the world, it is in much turmoil. Parts of it are still straining to follow the evil ways of the past, and are suffering greatly because of that recalcitrant attitude. Other parts of the world are tentatively testing the waters of Christ, to see if those waters might be the solution to the problems they are experiencing. And still other countries have jumped in feet first, body and soul, and are trying with all their might to bring their lives into conformity with the teachings of Christ. Everywhere, the evil nations of the past are breaking down, in spite of the best efforts of their governments to hold their wicked power structures together. As these events transpire, it will not be long before the Lord will have made a complete end of all nations in preparation for His millennial reign over all the earth.

Everything I knew, or thought I knew, has passed behind me. So much is new. The world has become a daily revelation of the wonderful good that can come, if only we will heed our Heavenly Father's will, for He loves us. Sin and rebellion once separated man from Him, but that now is all changed since the rebellious ones have been taken away, at least here in America. Zion now rises like the phoenix from the ashes of what once was.

It is becoming clear that God in His infinite wisdom, has used our checkered past to bless all who have followed Him. Even seemingly random events in human history have served to refine and strengthen us, slowly but surely preparing us for this time of restitution. Perhaps a parable expresses this idea best.

It is the parable of the mechanic. There was a master mechanic who built a beautiful car. It had within it everything one could desire to make it pleasing and useful. An enemy, seeing this marvelous vehicle, was jealous and came in the night, inflicting all manner of damage on the car. He slashed the seats, pulled out wires, dented the body and threw sand into the engine. In the morning, the master mechanic saw the damage. He grieved for the car and said within himself, "I will dismantle the car and clean it and fix it, and when I am through with it, it will be better than when I started." So he took the car apart. Each piece was carefully evaluated for what it needed. In his wisdom, some parts were fixed on site, but other parts were sent away to be repaired. Some of the repair shops were close and others were very far away. However, the mechanic was patient and was willing to wait in order that each part would get the best repair work possible. After many days, the work of repair and cleaning was done, and all that was bad was thrown out. Now, the master mechanic brought all of the pieces back together and rebuilt his beautiful car. Indeed, it was even better than before, for each part had been strengthened during the repairs. As for the enemy, the master mechanic had him thrown into prison where he could not harm the car anymore.

As with the car, the refined works of God's hands are all being brought back together again. We are witnesses to the wondrous changes, even multitudes of changes that are cascading through time to achieve that end that was known from the beginning. Changes, flowing in limitless variety, marching forward, sometimes dissonant, sometimes harmonious. Each change brings us through the process of endless interaction to see ourselves for who we really are, until in the end, each person receives that which they are willing to receive, and accepts the will of Him who guides the river of history and life. Each moment of turbulence or calm represents the tutoring hand of a loving father, who ceaselessly seeks our good, ever ready to assist and even intercede on our behalf, if only we will listen. This river of life, with its sweeping bends, rapids and waterfalls, is known from beginning to end by our Father, who watches it like an omniscient bystander who has viewed the same river for eons unnumbered. Only to those on the river is the end unknown, until we round that last bend that brings the final goal in sight. So it is in America now, glimpses of the end are coming into view, slowly but surely as the dense foliage of the world's distractions fall away. Change, like repentance, is taking the world and man, back to where we began. Hopefully our hearts and minds are filled with the riches of life's experiences, riches which we will be able to draw upon for eternity. Much of what we will appreciate for the rest of eternity will depend on our daily experiences upon this river. In the midst of all this change stands our Father, who is the same always. It is He who anchors us in truth and gives us stability and peace as we navigate the teaching trials of the river. The river flows more peacefully now, set as it is upon the course of righteousness. Perhaps the words of this book will help us remember the turbulence of life that preceded this tranquil place. Such beauty came at a high price, but there was no other way.

The hope of a bright future now stands squarely before us. As I say farewell, I hope the timeless truths of life have been made more clear by the events of the last few years. I plead with my family, my friends and all who read this book to remember always from whence our blessings come. Know that Heavenly Father lives and has revealed His truths to us through his prophets, past and present. Know that He sent His Son to save mankind by His great atonement, and lead us back to heaven. Know that divine truth is absolute, and ultimately is the only way to achieve lasting peace and happiness. Any attempt to ignore divine truth will only result in sorrow. Know that it is only through Christ that all good gifts come to man, and it is by His power that we were preserved through this recent time of great trial. May your testimony of Christ grow that you may be strong in righteousness. May you keep His commandments that you may be blessed. Until we meet, farewell.

House Upon The Sand

Appendix A

This is a list of some of the original sources on the events that are to proceed the Second Coming of Jesus Christ. This list is by no means complete, but it will offer a good starting point on the topic. The events in the story line of this book are largely based on information from these books. I strongly encourage everyone to read these materials for themselves.

The best sources are the scriptures. I have written a few of these sources down according to the standard work where they can be found.

BIBLE:

ISAIAH -   This is one of the best books for information on the last days. For some of those prophecies see the following chapters: 2-5, 10-11, 13, 18, 24, 26-35, 48-49, 51-52, 54-55, 57, 59-66. Most of the major points in this book can be found in these chapters. One of the clearest English translations of Isaiah is the translation by Avraham Gileadi.

JEREMIAH - 3, 16, 23, 25, 30-33.
EZEKIEL - 11, 20, 34, 36-48.
DANIEL - 2, 7- 8, 10-12.
JOEL
AMOS
ZEPHENIAH

ZECHARIAH
MALACHI
MATTHEW - 13,24(JST), 25
LUKE - 17 (JST)
REVELATION - 6-20

BOOK OF MORMON - Another Testament of Jesus Christ
2 NEPHI 26- 30
JACOB 5
3 NEPHI 20-25
ETHER 2, 8

DOCTRINE AND COVENANTS:
Sections- 29,45,77,84,87,88,105,133

The next best sources of prophecies about the Second Coming come from the modern prophets of Jesus Christ. There are a number of books that have been written that present these revelations in a format that is logical and easy to understand. These books are quite well done and are well referenced. Other books catalogue huge numbers of prophecies by their original sources. The authors of all these books usually make comments, and these comments should be viewed with that understanding. The credibility of the prophecies mentioned within these books should be evaluated individually according to their separate sources. A few of these books are listed below:

THE COMING OF THE LORD
    by Gerald N. Lund
PROPHECY KEY TO THE FUTURE
    by Duane S. Crowther
SPIRITUAL SURVIVAL IN THE LAST DAYS
    by Blaine and Brenton Yorgason
PROPHECY AND MODERN TIMES
    by W. Cleon Skousen
WILFORD WOODRUFF'S JOURNAL EXCERPTS,
    Pioneer Press-SLC,Utah

Appendix A

Pages 179-183, 187-194
"...AS A THIEF IN THE NIGHT." by Roger K. Young
PREPARING AND PROTECTING THE SAINTS IN THE
LAST DAYS   by Arlene Kay Butler
DESOLATION AND DESTRUCTION IN THE LAST DAYS
by Arlene Kay Butler
ZION ESTABLISHED, THE SECOND COMING, AND
MILLENNIUM   by Arlene Kay Butler

There is a book that talks about some of the Indian legends about the White God, the Prophet, who visited the ancestors of many Indian tribes. It reveals a little of what some of their feelings are on the Second Coming. It is:

HE WALKED THE AMERICAS
by L. Taylor Hansen, Amherst Press - Amherst, WI 54406

A vision that is of interest is one received by Charles D. Evans, a Patriarch. It was published in 1893 in Volume 15 of *The Contributor* magazine.

Appendix B

THE AMERICAN DREAM?

Dream-like our cities stand
    desolate and still,
Dead monuments to the failures of a vanished nation
    and a selfish will.

Like ancient temples
    crumbling idols of steel,
Built to the vanity of a now silent people
    who would not, and then could not, feel.

By Mark Peterson

THE STORM

Peace, Peace let it be
comfort my heart
and don't let me see
the danger so far away-

Sunlit streets
and pleasure shops
with busy people
... and beggars-

Touch, Touch my eyes
and blind my perception
that I won't realize
how big the cloud on the mountain-

Houses and cars
and wives with the children
food on the table
... and ignored starvation-

But... Peace, Peace let it be
it can't be a dream
this peace that surrounds me,
but there's black thunder rolling-

Hallowed Universities
and scholars with books
science and truth
... and then abortion-

My eyes, My eyes can you see
don't tell me the truth!
like an angry bee
the whirlwind falls from the mountain-

Fun times
and vacation to Vegas
with tender loving
... but who is my wife?

Peace, Peace let it be
please stay with my heart
for my eyes cannot see
and my destruction is come-

Blackened streets, and empty shops
Desolate homes, and cars without children
Empty classrooms, and science without truth
Stony silence, and an empty heart...

My heart, my heart now I know
that truth was my dream
and reality, my deception
and the storm, my end.

By Mark Peterson

SONRISE

The night draws late
  the moon is gone,
The darkness deepens
  before the dawn,

And evil men
  dark webs do spin,
Whose blackened threads
  catch most in sin,

But then we see
  On horizon's line
A morning star
  with hope to shine,

It speaks to eyes
  who wish to see,
The way to go
  to be set free,

It heralds the Son
  more brightly come,
To lead our walk
  and righteous run,

Alas, the crowd
  with dark entwined,
Reject the light
  ignore the sign,

For those who love
  the web's embrace,
Will stay behind
  in darkening place,

Until too late
  the price they pay,
And forfeit life
  in sin's dark way,

It's living, they thought
  but each strand a lie,
No safety there
  for all did die,

But those set free
  by the Son's new light,
Found peace in life
  from truth's great might,

The hoped for day
  now in man's sight,
A thousand years
  of truth and right.